CW01189178

Alladine and Palomides, Interior, and The Death of Tintagiles; Three Little Dramas for Marionettes

You are holding a reproduction of an original work that is in the public domain in the United States of America, and possibly other countries. You may freely copy and distribute this work as no entity (individual or corporate) has a copyright on the body of the work. This book may contain prior copyright references, and library stamps (as most of these works were scanned from library copies). These have been scanned and retained as part of the historical artifact.

This book may have occasional imperfections such as missing or blurred pages, poor pictures, errant marks, etc. that were either part of the original artifact, or were introduced by the scanning process. We believe this work is culturally important, and despite the imperfections, have elected to bring it back into print as part of our continuing commitment to the preservation of printed works worldwide. We appreciate your understanding of the imperfections in the preservation process, and hope you enjoy this valuable book.

MODERN PLAYS

EDITED BY
R. BRIMLEY JOHNSON
AND
N. ERICHSEN

Authorised Translation
All Rights Reserved

ALLADINE AND PALOMIDES, INTERIOR AND THE DEATH OF TINTAGILES
THREE LITTLE DRAMAS FOR MARIONETTES BY MAURICE MAETERLINCK

LONDON
DUCKWORTH & CO.
3 HENRIETTA STREET, W.C.
MDCCCXCIX

L.199467

INTRODUCTION

THESE three little plays were written five years ago; after Pelleas and Melisande, before the "Treasure of the Humble," before "Aglavaine and Selysette." They were the last of the series that began with "The Princess Maleine": a series of what might almost be termed Dramas of Unconsciousness and Instinct. A curious fatalism runs through them all; we feel that the men and women before us are merely unravelling the web that Destiny has spun round their lives—Destiny being a mysterious and inexorable force whose behests they must blindly obey. They are the slaves of their passions, slaves of the events that befall them; they are primitive beings, the mainspring of whose action lies forever exposed on the surface; they are creatures in whom deed follows instinctively on thought—and yet are we curiously conscious the while of the struggle in their soul, of their vague and helpless desire, as fate hurries them swiftly along to their doom. In his later work, M. Maeterlinck has entered fields of speculation that are wider, surer, nearer to life; here he seems still to be groping, searching, eagerly trying to discover the relationship that exists between man and his destiny, between man and the universe. These plays are often termed "mystic"; it were more correct, perhaps, to describe them as plays that are governed by obscure ideas, ideas that have not yet become clear; and, considering them thus, we shall

INTRODUCTION

find in them the germ of many a lofty, magnificent thought of "Wisdom and Destiny"; we shall understand the process of reasoning by which Fate, that in "Alladine and Palomides" is a monstrous force, crushing all life and all hope, shall in a few years be looked on as a power that can never enter the soul, uncalled; that can vanquish the upright man only by the good it compels him to do, and that has but one sword wherewith to attack him, the sword of goodness and truth.

"Three little dramas for marionettes," the legend runs on the title-page; nor is this a mere fanciful description of their nature, or affectation on the part of the author. He does but thereby give expression to his feeling that the naivete of treatment, the simplicity of character, render them somewhat ill-adapted for performance on the regular stage. And indeed few concessions are made to the realism demanded by modern convention. We know nothing of his people, who they are, or whence they come. This man is a king, that other a prince's son, the third a retainer. Often, indeed, they will be nameless—merely strangers, old men, sisters. They live, always, in palaces with gloomy corridors, and lofty, ruined towers; there are underground rivers, savage mountains, ominous forests; and the unquiet, restless sea is never far away. When the curtain rises, the characters are "discovered," and begin to speak; having said their say, they go out "by different ways," and the curtain abruptly falls. The environment is unchangiug, but it is because the poet wills it so, because he chooses the scene that appears to him best fitted to his subject, and persists in regarding the setting as a matter entirely subordinate. His methods, therefore, are by no means in harmony

INTRODUCTION

with those of the modern stage; and yet such pieces of his as have been performed—notably "Pelleas and Melisande,"—conclusively prove that these methods do not detract from the complete enjoyment of the audience. For M. Maeterlinck is a dramatist of rare quality; and plays, after all, are meant to be acted.

"Alladine and Palomides" has much in common with the play mentioned above, which was its immediate predecessor; though it perhaps fails to reach the very high level of that most exquisite tragedy. But yet it would seem in some measure to mark a fuller creativeness, a somewhat wider conception. Alladine is as naïve as Melisande, as unconscious, and yet more alert, more alive; endowed with more will and initiative, more foresight, more knowledge. Melisande shrinks from death, is scarcely aware of what death may mean; Alladine prefers love to life; and through all her childishness and want of reason we detect an ardent, urgent soul. And in this play, too, there is Astolaine—no less instinctive than the others—but whose instincts all make for nobility, sacrifice, devotion; whose love is so great that she can almost cheerfully resign the man she adores to a rival, and for this rival have only love too, and sisterly sympathy. Astolaine—to use a phrase of which M. Maeterlinck is fond—has attained the higher unconsciousness, that has drawn near unto God. She moves in the midst of these impetuous, impulsive creatures like one inspired, a centre of light; and we feel that her love, that is so hushed and silent, is yet infinitely greater and deeper than the more turbulent, overwhelming passion of Alladine. The old King who has grown weary of the monotony of his existence, and climbs on to the battlements to summon

INTRODUCTION

the events that are to rob him of reason and life, embodies an idea that will be familiar to the readers of M. Maeterlinck's essays. He was not able to understand the happiness that dwelt in the very uniformity of his existence; he clamoured for adventure; but, when it came, he lacked the power to transform it into consciousness, he allowed it to assume complete mastery over him and promptly yielded himself over to calamity. In marked contrast to Ablamore is the sage in "Intérieur"; the wise, benevolent old man, who places the centre of his joys in those about him, and finds happiness in watching their simple gestures, their calm and placid lives. "Intérieur" is a triumph of technical skill; as we read, we are painfully conscious of that peaceful family in their room, behind the lighted windows, seated there in all tranquillity, suspecting nothing; we dread the terrible awakening, and in our hearts are grateful to Mary for her suggestion that the sorrowful tale be not told until the morrow; and when at length the old man enters and the father rises to greet him, we almost turn our eyes away from the poignant misery that we know must ensue. And yet all is suggested only; there is not a word of despair. But this beautiful little play does more than merely stir our emotions; there is not a word that falls from the old man's lips but is noble, touching, throbbing with love, deeply and humanly sensitive; he is wise with a wisdom that disdains nothing, but has ever kept in close kinship with man. "The Death of Tintagiles"—the play M. Maeterlinck himself prefers of all he has written—is a strangely powerful study of sisterly love. Ygraine's devotion to little Tintagiles is all-absorbing, overwhelming; Ygraine herself, in her despair, her pathetic entreaty,

INTRODUCTION

her desperate struggle, is surely one of the most piteous victims of the cruelty of Fate. We have here the story of a child whom death tears away from his sister's helpless embrace; the play itself being symbolic of the struggle of all mankind against Death.

I have said that this play is symbolic; yet are those doubtless mistaken who imagine that there is scarcely a line in M. Maeterlinck's writings but has its special cryptic meaning. Symbolism there certainly is, but it is broad and general; one central idea, or set of ideas, will govern the whole; the plays however are invariably simple and direct, and by no means underlined with constant symbolic reference. The air, it may be, is charged with mystery; but only such as pertains to the shadowy twilight in which the characters move, and have being. Let us take, as an instance, the scene in "Alladine and Palomides," where the two lovers are imprisoned in the grotto; they tear the bandages off their eyes, and the light thrown up by the blue water that flows at their feet reveals to them countless sparkling jewels and radiant flowers on the walls of the cavern; yet it needs but one ray of the sun, as it pierces through the cleft in the rock, to prove that what seemed flashing gem is nothing but dull and lifeless stone; what seemed exquisite roses only moist and decaying fungus. Here we may find perhaps some connection with the thought M. Maeterlinck has since expressed in his essays, viz., that the beautiful dream which shrinks from reality, actuality, and cannot support the steady light of everyday life, is in itself a tawdry thing too, and unreal, and not what it seems. But those unable to define this wider and more general meaning will still

INTRODUCTION

understand the scene in the grotto as fully and completely as the others; they will understand as Alladine and Palomides understood. There are many, too, who will ponder over the symbolic meaning of Alladine's pet lamb, that fled from her and was found dead where she herself met her death; many will be eager to know who the mysterious queen may be, who so ruthlessly persecutes Tintagiles; yet will those, perhaps, appreciate these little plays the most who will be content to take them as they are, demanding no definition, seeking for no hidden meaning; who will be satisfied to accept what the author gives them, and try to fathom only the spirit that underlies his work. For we have here little dramas of life, viewed through a darkened mirror; life shorn of its complexity, reduced to its primal simplicity. They are studies in monochrome, wherein many of the subtler half-tones do yet find expression; they are things of delicate and tender beauty—whereof much, alas, must inevitably be lost in process of translation; and finally they are the creation of a lofty and penetrating mind, that handles all things with reverence and invests them with dignity; a mind that in all existing things sees matter for admiration and wonder.

ALFRED SUTRO.

THE translations of *Interior* and *The Death of Tintagiles*, revised for this series by Messrs WILLIAM ARCHER and ALFRED SUTRO respectively, have been reprinted with the kind permission of Mr ARCHIBALD GROVE, Mr HEINEMANN and Messrs HENRY & Co., from the *New Review* of November 1894, and the *Pageant* of December 1896.

EDD.

ALLADINE AND PALOMIDES

TRANSLATED BY ALFRED SUTRO

CHARACTERS

Ablamore.
Astolaine, *Ablamore's daughter*.
Alladine.
Palomides.
The Sisters of Palomides.
A Doctor.

ACT I

Scene

A wild spot in the gardens.

ALLADINE *lies asleep;* ABLAMORE *is bending over her.*

ABLAMORE.

Sleep seems to reign here, day and night, beneath these trees. No sooner have we arrived, she and I, towards eventide, no sooner has she seated herself, than sleep steals over her. . . . Alas, I ought to be glad of it! For in the daytime, if I speak to her and our eyes chance to meet, there comes into her eyes a look so hard that she might be a slave whom I had ordered to do a thing that could not be done. . . But that look is not usual with her. Often and often have I watched those beautiful eyes as they rested on children, the forest, the sea, or whatever was near. At me she smiles as we smile at our enemies; and never dare I bend over her save when her eyes can no longer behold me. A few such moments are mine every evening; the rest of the day I live by her side with my face averted. . . It is sad to love too late. . . Women do not understand that years cannot separate heart from heart. "The wise King" they used to call me. I was wise because, till then, nothing had happened. There are some men from whom events do thus seem to shrink, and turn aside. Nothing would ever take place where I chanced to be. . . I had some suspicion of this in bygone days. There were friends of mine, in my youth, who had only to show themselves for adventures to flock to them; but if I sallied forth in their midst, seeking gladness or sorrow, we would ever return empty handed. . . It is as though I had paralysed destiny; and there was a time when this was a source of much pride to me. . . During my reign, all men have known peace. . . But now I have come to believe that even disaster is better than lethargy, and that there must be a life that is loftier, more stirring, than this constant lying in wait. . . They shall see that I too, when I choose, have the power to stir up the dead water that slumbers in the mighty tarn of the future. . . Alladine, Alladine! . . . Oh how beautiful she is! Her long hair falls on to the flowers, on to her lamb; her mouth is half open, and fresher than the dawn. . . I will kiss her—she shall not know: I will keep back this poor white beard of mine . . . (*he kisses her*)—She smiled. . . Why should I be sorry for her? She gives me a few years of her life, but some day she will reign as queen; and before I wend my way hence, I shall at least have done a little good. . . They will be surprised. . . She herself knows nothing. . . Ah see, she awakes, in alarm. Where do you come from, Alladine?

ALLADINE.

I have had a bad dream.

ACT I.   PALOMIDES

ABLAMORE.

What is it? Why look you out yonder?

ALLADINE.

Someone has passed by, on the road.

ABLAMORE.

I heard nothing. . .

ALLADINE.

I tell you someone is coming. . . There he is! (*She points to a young cavalier who is advancing towards them through the trees holding his horse by the bridle.*) Do not hold my hand; I am not frightened. . . He has not seen us. . .

ABLAMORE.

Who would dare to come here? . . . If I were not sure. . . I believe it is Palomides. . . He is betrothed to Astolaine. . . See, he raises his head. . . Is it you, Palomides?

Enter PALOMIDES.

PALOMIDES.

Yes, my father . . . if I may already call you by that name. I have come before the day and before the hour. . .

ABLAMORE.

You are welcome, whatever the hour. . . But what can have happened? We did not expect you so soon, not for at least two days. . . Has Astolaine come with you?

PALOMIDES.

No; she will arrive to-morrow. We have travelled day and night. She was tired; she begged me to go on before her. . . Are my sisters here?

ABLAMORE.

They came three days ago, and wait for the wedding. You look very happy, Palomides.

PALOMIDES.

Who would not be happy, that had found all he sought? There was a time when sorrow weighed on me. But now the days seem lighter to me, and more gentle, than the innocent birds that come and nestle in our hand. And if by chance one of the old moments returns to me, I have but to draw nigh unto Astolaine, and a window would seem to fly open and let in the dawn. Astolaine's soul can be seen; it is there; it takes you in its arms and comforts you, without saying a word, as one comforts a suffering child. . . I shall never understand . . I know not whence it arises; but my knees bend under me if I only speak of her. . .

ALLADINE.

I want to go in.

ABLAMORE (*noticing that Alladine and Palomides are looking shyly at each other*).

This is little Alladine, who has come from the depths of Arcady. . . Take each other by the hand. . . You are surprised, Palomides?

ACT I. PALOMIDES

PALOMIDES.

My father. . .
  [*His horse makes a brusque movement which startles Alladine's lamb.*]

ABLAMORE.

Be careful; your horse has frightened Alladine's lamb. It will run away.

ALLADINE.

No; it never runs away. It was surprised, that is all. It is a lamb that my godmother gave me. . . It is not like other lambs. It never leaves me, day or night.
  [*She caresses the lamb.*

PALOMIDES (*also caressing it*).

It is looking at me with the eyes of a child.

ALLADINE.

It understands everything.

ABLAMORE.

It is time for you to go to your sisters, Palomides. They will be surprised to see you.

ALLADINE.

They have gone to the cross-roads every day. I went with them; but they did not expect so soon. . .

ABLAMORE.

Come, Palomides is covered with dust and must be tired. We have too much to tell one another, we must not stay here. To-morrow we will talk. The dawn, they say, is wiser than evening. See, the palace gates are open and seem to invite us. . .

ALLADINE.

I cannot tell why it is that uneasiness comes to me, each time I go into the palace. It is so vast and I am so little; I am lost in it. . . . And all those windows that look on to the sea. . . . You cannot count them. . . . And the corridors that wind, and wind, for no reason; and others that do not turn, but that lose themselves in the walls. . . . And the rooms I dare not go into—

PALOMIDES.

We will go into every one. . . .

ALLADINE.

I feel that I was not meant to live there, or that it was not built for me. . . Once, I lost my way. . . . I had to open thirty doors before the daylight returned to me. And I could not escape; the last door led to a lake. . . And there are vaults that are cold even in summer; and galleries that twist, and twist, back on to themselves. And stairs that lead no whither and terraces whence nothing can be seen. . .

ABLAMORE.

How you speak to-night, you who are always so silent. . .
[*They go out.*

ACT II. SC. I.   **PALOMIDES**

ACT II

Scene I

ALLADINE *is discovered, her forehead pressed against one of the windows looking on to the park.* Enter ABLAMORE.

ABLAMORE.

Alladine.

ALLADINE (*turning round quickly*).

Yes.

ABLAMORE.

Oh how pale you look! Are you ill?

ALLADINE.

No.

ABLAMORE.

What were you looking at in the park? At the row of fountains in front of the windows? They are marvellous, indefatigable. They sprang up, one after the other, at the death of each of my daughters. . . . At night I can hear them singing in the garden. They recall to me the lives they stand for, and I am able to distinguish their voices. . .

ALLADINE.

I know. . .

ABLAMORE.

You must forgive me; I repeat myself at times; my memory is not quite so faithful. . It is not because of my age; I am not an old man yet, thank

God; but a King has a thousand cares. Palomides has been telling me of his adventures. . .

ALLADINE.

Ah!

ABLAMORE.

He has not acted in all things as he would have desired to act. Young men are not very strong-willed, nowadays.—I was surprised. There were countless suitors for my daughter's hand; I had chosen him from among them all. She needed a soul that should be no less profound than her own. Nothing that he has done could be called inexcusable, but yet I had hoped for more. . . What impression did he make on you?

ALLADINE.

Who?

ABLAMORE.

Palomides.

ALLADINE.

I have only seen him that one evening. . .

ABLAMORE.

I was astonished.—Hitherto all has gone well with him. He undertook nothing that he did not accomplish successfully, and without many words. He always could overcome danger, with scarcely an effort; while so many others can hardly open a door without finding death crouching behind. He was of those upon whom events seem to wait, on their knees. But of late it appears as though something were

ACT II. SC. I. **PALOMIDES**

broken; as though his star were no longer the same; as though every step that he took dragged him further away from himself.—I know not what it can be.—He himself seems not to suspect it; but to everyone else it is clear. . . But enough of all this; see, the night is coming towards us, creeping over the walls. Shall we go together to the wood of Astolat, where we always spend our evenings?

ALLADINE.

I shall not go out to-night.

ABLAMORE.

We will stay here then, since you prefer it. But the air is tender to-night; the evening is beautiful. (*Alladine trembles, unperceived by him.*) I have had flowers planted along the hedges; I should have liked to have shown them to you. . .

ALLADINE.

No, not to-night. . . I beg of you. . . I like going there with you. . . the air is very pure, and the trees . . . but not to-night. . . (*she bursts into tears, and nestles close to the old man's breast*). I am not well. . .

ABLAMORE.

Not well? You are falling. . . I will call. . .

ALLADINE.

No, no . . . it is nothing . . . it is over now. . .

ALLADINE AND ACT II. SC. II.

ABLAMORE.

Sit down. Wait. . . .

[*He goes quickly to the door at the back, and throws it wide open. Palomides is behind, seated on a bench that faces the door; he has not had time to turn his eyes away. Ablamore looks fixedly at him, but says not a word; then returns to the room. Palomides rises, and steals away through the corridor, on tiptoe. The lamb goes out of the room, unperceived by the others.*

SCENE II

A drawbridge over the palace moat. Palomides enters at one end, Alladine at the other, with her lamb by her side. King Ablamore is leaning out of a window in the tower.

PALOMIDES.

You are going out, Alladine?—I have just returned; I have been hunting. . . There has been a shower. . .

ALLADINE.

I have never yet crossed this bridge.

PALOMIDES.

It leads to the forest. People seldom pass over it. They prefer to take another road, which is much longer. I imagine that they are afraid, because the dykes here are deeper than elsewhere; and the black water that pours from the mountain seethes horribly between the walls before it throws itself into the sea. It is always angry, but the quays are so high that one

ACT II. SC. II.   **PALOMIDES**

scarcely can see it. This is the most deserted wing of the palace. But the forest is more beautiful this side—older and grander than anything you ever have seen, full of strange trees and flowers that have sprung up of themselves. Will you come?

ALLADINE.

I don't know. . . I am afraid of the angry water.

PALOMIDES.

Come—there is no cause for its anger. See, your lamb is looking at me as though it desired to go. Come. . .

ALLADINE.

Do not call, it will break away from me. . .

PALOMIDES.

Come with me. Come. . .

[*The lamb escapes from Alladine and bounds towards Palomides; but it stumbles on the slope of the drawbridge, misses its footing and falls into the moat.*

ALLADINE.

Where is it? What has happened?

PALOMIDES.

It has fallen into the moat! It is struggling in the whirlpool. Do not look; nothing can be done. . .

ALLADINE.

You will save it?

PALOMIDES.

Save it! Alas, it is already drawn under. Yet an instant and it will be below, underneath the vaults; and God Himself will never behold it again. . .

ALLADINE.

Leave me! leave me!

PALOMIDES.

What have I done?

ALLADINE.

Leave me! I never want to see you again. . .

[*Ablamore enters abruptly, seizes Alladine and takes her away quickly, without saying a word.*

SCENE III

A room in the palace.

ABLAMORE *and* ALLADINE *are discovered together.*

ABLAMORE.

See, Alladine, my hands are not trembling, and my heart beats as tranquilly as that of a sleeping child, and indeed my voice has never been raised in anger. I do not blame Palomides, though his conduct may well seem unpardonable. And as for you, why should I blame you? You obey laws that you know not of; nor could you have acted otherwise. I shall say not a word of all that took place, but a few days ago, by the side of the castle moat, or of what the sudden death of the lamb might have revealed to me, had I

ACT II. SC. III.   **PALOMIDES**

>chosen to believe in omens. But last night I witnessed the kiss you exchanged beneath the windows of Astolaine's room. At that moment I happened to be with her. The one great dread of her soul is lest she disturb the happiness of those about her by a tear, or even a quiver of the eyelid; and thus I never shall know whether she also beheld that miserable kiss. But I do know how deeply she can suffer. I shall ask nothing of you that you cannot confess to me; all I wish you to tell me is whether you obeyed some secret plan when you followed Palomides underneath the window where you must have seen us. Answer me fearlessly; you know I have already forgiven.

ALLADINE.

I did not kiss him.

ABLAMORE.

What! you did not kiss Palomides, or he you?

ALLADINE.

No.

ABLAMORE.

>Ah! . . . Listen: I came hither prepared to forgive all that had happened: I said to myself that you had acted as most of us act when our soul holds aloof from us. . . But now all must be told. You love Palomides: you kissed him before my eyes.

ALLADINE.

No.

ABLAMORE.

Do not run away. I am only an old man. Do not try to escape.

ALLADINE.
I am not trying to escape. . .
ABLAMORE.
Ah! Ah! That is because you imagine these old hands of mine are powerless! There is strength enough in them still to tear out a secret, wheresoever it be. (*He seizes her by the arms*) There is strength enough in them still to combat those you prefer . . . (*He forces her arms behind her head.*) Ah, you refuse to speak! But the moment will come when the pain will force your soul to rush forth, like clear water. . . .
ALLADINE.
No, no!
ABLAMORE.
Again? We are not at the end, then; the road is long; and truth is ashamed, and hides behind the rocks. . . Is it coming? . . . I see it moving in your eyes; I feel its soft breath on my cheek. . . Oh Alladine, Alladine! (*he suddenly releases her*) I heard your bones lament, like little children. . . I have not hurt you? . . . Do not kneel to me—it is I who must go on my knees before you. . . I am a monster. . . . Have pity. . . It is not for myself alone that I have besought this of you. . . I have only this one poor daughter. . . The others are dead. . . . Once there were seven around me. . . They were beautiful, radiant with joy, I have never seen them again. . . The only one who was left to me was also about to die. . . She had no desire to live. . . . Then there was a sudden, unexpected meeting,

ACT II. SC. IV.   **PALOMIDES**

and I saw she no longer craved for death. . . I ask nothing impossible of you. . .
> [*Alladine weeps, but makes no answer.*

Scene IV

Astolaine's room

ASTOLAINE *and* PALOMIDES *are discovered.*

PALOMIDES.

Astolaine, when it so fell about that I met you, some few months ago, I seemed at last to have found what I had sought for many years. Till then, I had no suspicion of all that real goodness meant, its sweetness and tenderness; I was blind to the perfect simplicity of a truly beautiful soul. And these things stirred me so deeply that it seemed to be the first time in my life that I stood before a human being. I seemed to have spent all my days in an airless chamber; and it was you who flung open the door — and I knew then what other men's souls must be, what my soul, too, might become. . . . Since then, I have drawn closer to you. I have seen the things that you did; and others, too, have spoken of you.

There were evenings when I wandered away from you, silently, and sought a secluded spot in the palace, and could not keep back my tears as I thought of you, and wondered; though you only had raised your eyes, it may be, or made some little unconscious gesture, or smiled, perhaps, for no visible reason, and yet at the very moment that the souls around you craved for this smile, and needed it, for their comfort. You alone know of these moments; for it would seem that your soul contains the soul of each one of us; and I cannot believe that those who have not drawn near to you can tell what the true life may be. And I speak of all this to-day because I feel that I never shall be what I had hoped that I might become... Fate has stepped out towards me; or I, it may be, have beckoned to Fate; for we never know whether we ourselves have gone forth or Fate have come seeking us—something has happened whereby my eyes have been opened, at the very moment that we were about to draw unhappiness down on us; and I recognised that there must be a power more incomprehensible than the beauty of the most beautiful face, the most beautiful soul; and mightier too, since I must perforce give way to it... I know not whether you understand... In that case, pity me... I have said to myself all that could be said... I know what it is that I lose; I know that her soul is the soul of a child, of a poor and helpless child, by the side of your soul: and for all that I cannot resist...

ASTOLAINE.

Do not weep... I too am well aware that we are not always able to do the thing we prefer... I was not unprepared for your coming... There must indeed be laws mightier than those of the soul, whereof we forever are speaking.. (*she suddenly kisses him*)—But I love you the more for it, my poor Palomides. . .

PALOMIDES.

I love you, too . . . more than her whom I love. . . Are you crying, too?

ASTOLAINE.

They are little tears . . . let them not sadden you. . . . My tears fall because I am a woman; but women's tears, they say, are not painful. . . See, my eyes are already dry . . . I was well aware of it . . . I knew I should soon be awakened. . . And now that it is over I can breathe more freely, for I am no longer happy. . . That is all. . . We must consider what had best be done, for you and for her. I am afraid my father suspects. . .

[*They go out.*

ACT III

SCENE I

An apartment in the palace.

ABLAMORE *is discovered.* ASTOLAINE *is standing on the threshold of a half-opened door at the end of the room.*

ASTOLAINE.

Father, I have come to you in obedience to a voice within me that I can no longer resist. You know all that took place in my soul when I met Palomides. He seemed different from other men... To-day I come to you seeking your help... for I know not what I had best say to him... I have realised that I cannot love... It is not he who has changed, but I—or perhaps I did not understand... And since it is impossible for me to love the man I had selected from among them all with the love I had dreamed of, it must needs be that these things cannot touch my heart... I know it now... My eyes shall no longer stray to the paths of love; and you will see me living by your side without sorrow and without disquiet... I feel that I am about to be happy...

ABLAMORE.

Come nearer to me, Astolaine. It was not thus that in days gone by you were wont to speak to your father. You stand there, on the threshold of a half-closed door, as though anxious to fly from me; you keep your hand on the key, as though you desired forever to hide from me the secret of your heart. You know full well that I have not understood what you have said to me; that words have no meaning when soul is not near unto soul. Come closer to me—you need tell me no more. (*Astolaine approaches slowly.*) There comes a moment when soul meets soul; when all is known to them though the lips remain closed. ... Come closer, closer still... They are even yet too far apart, these souls of ours—their light is so feeble around us! (*Astolaine suddenly halts.*) You are afraid ?—You know how far one may go ? —Then it is I will come to you... (*He moves*

ACT III. SC. II. **PALOMIDES**

slowly towards Astolaine, stands in front of her and gazes fixedly at her.) I see you, Astolaine. . .

ASTOLAINE.

Father! . . . (*She bursts into tears and sobs in the old man's breast.*)

ABLAMORE.

You see how useless it was. . .

SCENE II

A room in the palace.

Enter ALLADINE *and* PALOMIDES.

PALOMIDES.

To-morrow all will be ready. We must not wait any longer. He is wandering like a madman through the palace corridors; I met him but a short time ago. He looked at me, but said nothing; I passed on, but, when I turned round, I saw that he was laughing to himself and flourishing a bunch of keys. When he saw that I was watching him, he nodded, and smiled, and tried to look friendly. He must be nursing some secret scheme—we are in the hands of a master whose reason is tottering. To-morrow we shall be far away. Out yonder there are wonderful countries that are more like your own. Astolaine has already prepared for our flight and for that of my sisters. . .

ALLADINE.

What did she say?

PALOMIDES.

Nothing, nothing . . . We shall be on the sea for days, then days of forest—and afterwards we shall come to the lakes and mountains that surround my father's castle; and you will see how different they are from everything here, where the sky is like the roof of a cavern and the black trees are done to death by the storms. . . Ours is a sky beneath which none are afraid; our forests are full of life, and with us the flowers never close. . .

ALLADINE.

Did she cry?

PALOMIDES.

Why these questions? . . . That is a thing of which we have no right to speak—do you hear? Her life has nothing in common with our poor life; love must perforce be silent before it dare approach her. . . When I think of her, we seem to be beggars, you and I, and clothed in rags. . . Leave me, leave me! . . . For I could say things to you . . .

ALLADINE.

Palomides! . . . What has happened?

PALOMIDES.

Go, go. . . . I saw tears that came not from the eyes, but from far beyond. . . . For there are other things . . . And yet we are right, perhaps; but oh God, if that be so how sorry I am to be right! . . . Go, go. . . . I will tell you to-morrow, to-morrow, to-morrow. . .   [*They go out by different ways.*

ACT III. SC. III. **PALOMIDES**

SCENE III

A corridor in front of Alladine's room.

Enter ASTOLAINE *and the* SISTERS OF PALOMIDES.

ASTOLAINE.

The horses are waiting in the forest, but Palomides refuses to fly, although your lives are in peril as well as his own. I no longer recognise my poor father. He has a fixed idea which unhinges his reason. I have been following him, the last three days, step by step, crouching behind walls and pillars, for he will suffer no one to accompany him. To-day, with the first rays of dawn, he again set forth and wandered through the rooms of the palace, and the corridors, and along the moat and the ramparts, waving the great golden keys he has had made, and chanting loudly the strange song whose refrain, "Go where your eyes may lead," may perhaps have reached you even in your rooms. Hitherto I have told you nothing of all this, for these are things whereof one should not speak without cause. He must have confined Alladine in this room, but no one knows what he has done to her. I have watched every night, and run to the door, and listened, the moment he had turned away, but I have heard not a sound in the room. . . Can you hear anything?

ONE OF THE SISTERS OF PALOMIDES.

Only the murmur of the air as it passes through the crevice in the wall. . .

ALLADINE AND ACT III. SC. III.

ANOTHER SISTER.

When I listen I seem only to hear the great pendulum, as it swings to and fro. . .

A THIRD SISTER.

But who is this little Alladine, and why is he so angry with her?

ASTOLAINE.

She is a little Greek slave, who has come from the depths of Arcady. . . He is not angry with her, but. . . Hark, there he is. (*Someone is heard singing in the distance.*) Hide behind these pillars. He has given orders that no one should pass along this corridor. (*They hide. Ablamore comes in, singing, and flourishing a great bunch of keys.*)

ABLAMORE (*sings*).

Unhappiness had three keys of gold
—But the queen is not yet freed—
Unhappiness had three keys of gold
Go where your eyes may lead.

[*He seems terribly weary and lets himself fall on to the bench that faces Alladine's room; for some little time still he murmurs his song, then falls asleep, his hands hanging down by his side and his head sinking on to his shoulder.*

ASTOLAINE.

Come; and make no noise. He has fallen asleep on the bench. Oh my poor father! How white his hair has grown these last few days! He is so unhappy,

ACT III. SC. III.   **PALOMIDES**

so weak, that even sleep can bring no comfort to him. For three whole days I have not dared look into his face. . .

ONE OF THE SISTERS OF PALOMIDES.

He sleeps profoundly. . .

ASTOLAINE.

Yes; but one can see that his soul is not at rest. . . The sun is beating down on his eyes. . . I will draw his cloak over his face. . .

ANOTHER SISTER.

No, no, do not touch him; you might startle him, wake him.

ASTOLAINE.

There is someone coming along the corridor. . . Do you stand in front of him, and hide him. . . It would not be right that a stranger should behold him thus. . .

ONE OF THE SISTERS.

It is Palomides. . .

ASTOLAINE.

I will cover up those poor eyes. . . (*She spreads the cloak over Ablamore's face.*) Palomides must not see him like this. . . He is too unhappy . . .

Enter PALOMIDES.

PALOMIDES.

What has happened?

ONE OF THE SISTERS.

He has fallen asleep on the bench.

PALOMIDES.

He could not see me, but I have been following him. . .
    He has said nothing?

ASTOLAINE.

No; but see how he has suffered. . .

PALOMIDES.

Has he the keys?

ANOTHER SISTER.

He is holding them in his hand.

PALOMIDES.

I will take them from him.

ASTOLAINE.

What do you mean to do? Oh be careful—do not wake
    him. For three nights now he has been roaming
    through the palace. . .

PALOMIDES.

I will unclasp his hand gently—he will not feel it. We
    dare not wait any longer. God alone can tell what
    he has done! He will forgive us when his reason
    returns. . . Oh! how weak his hands are!

ASTOLAINE.

Be careful—oh be careful!

PALOMIDES.

I have the keys—which one is it? I will open the door.

ONE OF THE SISTERS.

I am frightened—do not open it yet . . . Palomides. . .

ACT III. SC. III.   **PALOMIDES**

PALOMIDES.

Stay here. . . I know not what I shall find. . .
 [*He goes to the door, opens it, and enters the room.*

ASTOLAINE.

Is she there?

PALOMIDES (*from within the room*).

I can see nothing—the shutters are closed. . .

ASTOLAINE.

Be careful, Palomides. . . Let me go first. . . Your voice is trembling. . .

PALOMIDES.

No, no . . . a ray of sunlight is stealing through the chinks of the shutters. . .

ONE OF THE SISTERS.

Yes—the sun is shining brightly outside.

PALOMIDES (*suddenly emerging from the room*).

Come, quickly!—I believe that she . . .

ASTOLAINE.

You have seen her? . . .

PALOMIDES.

She is lying on the bed. . . She does not move. . . I do not think that— . . . Come in!
 [*They all enter the room.*

ASTOLAINE AND THE SISTERS OF PALOMIDES (*inside the room*).

Here she is. . . . No, no, she is not dead. . . Alladine, Alladine! Oh, poor child. . . Do not scream. . . She has fainted. . . They have tied her hair round her mouth . . . and fastened her hands behind her . . . they are fastened with her hair. . . Alladine, Alladine! . . . Quick, get some water. . .

[*Ablamore has awakened and appears on the threshold.*

ASTOLAINE.

My father is there!

ABLAMORE (*going up to Palomides*).

Was it you who opened the door of this room?

PALOMIDES.

Yes, I—I did it—and then—and then? . . . I cannot let her die before my eyes. . . See what you have done. . . . Alladine! Be not afraid. . . She is opening her eyes. . . I will not endure . . .

ABLAMORE.

Do not speak so loudly. . . Come, let us open the shutters. . . . We cannot see, in here. . . Alladine. . . . Ah, she has already got up. . . Come you too, Alladine. . . Look, my children, how dark it is in the room. As dark as though we were thousands of feet underground. But I have only to open a shutter, and see! All the light of the sky, all the light of the sun! . . . It calls for no mighty effort—the light is eager enough. . . We have only to call—it will never fail to obey. . .

ACT IV.   PALOMIDES

Do you see the river out yonder, with the islands in its midst, all covered with flowers? The sky to-day might be a ring of crystal. . . Alladine, Palomides, look. . . Come nigh unto heaven, both of you. . . Kiss each other, with this new light upon you. . . I bear you no ill-will. You have done what was ordained; and so have I too. . . Lean for one instant out of this open window; look once again at the trees and the flowers. . .

[*A silence. He quietly closes the shutters.*

ACT IV

Scene

Vast subterranean grottoes.

ALLADINE *and* PALOMIDES *are discovered.*

PALOMIDES.

They have bandaged my eyes and bound my hands. . .

ALLADINE.

My hands are bound too, my eyes are bandaged. . . I believe my hands are bleeding. . .

PALOMIDES.

Wait, wait. Oh how grateful I am to-day for my strength. . . . I feel that the knots are giving. . . I will try once more, though I burst every vein. . . Once more still—ah, my hands are free! (*he tears off the bandage*) and my eyes too!

ALLADINE.

You can see?

PALOMIDES.

Yes.

ALLADINE.

Where are we?

PALOMIDES.

I cannot see you. . .

ALLADINE.

I am here, here. . .

PALOMIDES.

The tears still stream down my eyes from the effects of the bandage. . . We are not in darkness. . . Is it you that I hear, out yonder, close to the light?

ALLADINE.

I am here, come to me. . .

PALOMIDES.

You are on the edge of the light. Do not move; I cannot tell what there is all around you. My eyes still remember the bandage. They drew it so tight that my eyelids have nigh burst in twain.

ALLADINE.

Come quickly, the cords suffocate me. I can wait no longer. . . .

PALOMIDES.

I hear only a voice that comes forth from the light. . . .

ACT IV. **PALOMIDES**

ALLADINE.

Where are you?

PALOMIDES.

I know not... I am still groping in darkness... Speak again, that I may know where to look for you... You seem to be in the midst of infinite radiance...

ALLADINE.

Come to me, oh come! I have suffered in silence but now can endure it no longer...

PALOMIDES (*feeling his way along*).

Is that you? I thought you so far away! My tears had deceived me. But now I am here and can see you. Oh, your hands are wounded! The blood has dropped down from them on to your dress; the cords have sunk into your flesh. And I have nothing to cut them with—they have taken away my dagger. I must tear them off. Wait, wait—I have found the knots.

ALLADINE.

First take off this bandage which blinds me.

PALOMIDES.

I cannot... I am dazzled... I seem to be caught in the midst of innumerable threads of gold...

ALLADINE.

My hands, then, my hands!

PALOMIDES.

The cords are of silk... Wait, the knots are giving.

They have wound the cord round thirty times. . .
There, there!—Oh how your hands are bleeding! . . .
They look as though they were dead. . .

ALLADINE.

No, no, they live, they live! See! . . .
  [*No sooner are her hands freed than she flings them around Palomides' neck and embraces him passionately.*

PALOMIDES.

Alladine!

ALLADINE.

Palomides!

PALOMIDES.

Alladine, Alladine! . . .

ALLADINE.

I am happy now. . . I have waited so long! . . .

PALOMIDES.

I was afraid to come. . .

ALLADINE.

I am happy . . . I want to see you. . .

PALOMIDES.

They have fastened the bandage so tight that it might be a helmet of steel. . . Do not move; I have found the gold threads. . .

ALLADINE.

Yes, yes, I will move. . .
  [*She throws her arms round him, and kisses him again.*

ACT IV.   **PALOMIDES**

PALOMIDES.

Be careful. Do not turn round. I am afraid of hurting you...

ALLADINE.

Tear it off! Do not mind. There is nothing can hurt me now...

PALOMIDES.

I too want to see you...

ALLADINE.

Tear it off, tear it off! I am far beyond reach of pain! ... Tear it off! You do not know how gladly I would die.... Where are we?

PALOMIDES.

You will see, you will see... We are in the midst of innumerable grottoes ... there are great blue caverns, with shining pillars, and lofty arches...

ALLADINE.

Why do you answer when I speak to you?

PALOMIDES.

I care not where we are so we be but together...

ALLADINE.

Already you love me less...

PALOMIDES.

What do you mean?

ALLADINE.

Do I need to be told where I am, when it is on your

heart that I lie? . . . I beseech you, tear off the bandage! . . It shall not be like one who is blind that I enter your soul. . . What are you doing, Palomides? You do not laugh when I laugh, or cry when I cry. You do not clap your hands when I clap mine; you do not tremble when I speak and tremble in the depths of my heart. . . The bandage, the bandage! . . . I want to see! . . Tear it off, pull it over my hair! (*she tears off the bandage*). Oh! . . .

PALOMIDES.

You can see?

ALLADINE.

Yes, I see you . . . and only you. . .

PALOMIDES.

What is it, Alladine? Why are your kisses already so sorrowful?

ALLADINE.

Where are we?

PALOMIDES.

Why do you ask that so sadly?

ALLADINE.

I am not sad, but I scarcely can open my eyes. . .

PALOMIDES.

I feel as though your joy had fallen on my lips as a child might fall on the threshold of its father's house. . . Do not turn from me. . . I am afraid of your leaving me, afraid lest this all be a dream. . .

ACT IV.   **PALOMIDES**

ALLADINE.

Where are we?

PALOMIDES.

In the midst of caverns I never have seen. . . . Does it not seem as though more light were coming towards us?—When I opened my eyes all was dark; now, little by little, all seems to be clear to me. I have often heard of the marvellous caverns that lay beneath Ablamore's palace; these must be they. No one ever went into them; and only the King had the keys. I knew that the sea flooded those that lay deepest; and the light we behold is doubtless thrown up by the sea. . . They thought they were burying us in darkness. They came hither with lanterns and torches, and saw only blackness; but the light comes to us who have nothing. . . It grows brighter and brighter. . . It must be the dawn that is piercing the ocean, and sending us, through the green waves, all the purity of its innocent soul. . .

ALLADINE.

How long have we been here?

PALOMIDES.

I cannot tell. . . I had made no effort until I heard your voice. . .

ALLADINE.

I know not how it all happened. I was asleep in the room where you had found me; when I awoke my eyes were bound and my two hands tied to my belt. . .

PALOMIDES.

I too was asleep... I heard nothing, and before I could open my eyes the bandage was over them. I struggled fiercely, in the darkness, but they were stronger than I... They must have led me through deep-lying vaults, for I could feel the cold dripping on to my shoulders; I went down and down so long that I could not keep count of the steps... They said nothing to you?

ALLADINE.

Not a word. But I could hear that someone was weeping as he walked by my side; and then I fainted...

PALOMIDES (*kissing her*).

Alladine!

ALLADINE.

How gravely you kiss me...

PALOMIDES.

Do not close your eyes when I kiss you... I want to look into your heart and see my kisses quivering there, and the dew that steals up from your soul... never again shall we know such kisses as these...

ALLADINE.

Always, always!

PALOMIDES!

Not so; for our lips meet now over the bosom of death; and that can happen but once... Oh, you are beautiful thus!... It is the first time that I have been near to you, that I have looked into your eyes. . . It is strange; people pass by each other and think they have seen; yet how does everything change the moment the lips have met. . . There; do as you will. . . I stretch out my arms to admire you as though you no longer were mine; then I bring them together until I again meet your kiss, and I see only joy everlasting. . . We needed this unearthly light! . . . (*He kisses her again.*) Ah! what have you done? Be careful; we are on the crest of a rock that hangs over the light-giving water. Do not move. It was time. . . Do not turn round too quickly. I was dazzled. . .

ALLADINE (*turning and looking at the blue water whence the light is thrown up*).
Oh! . . .

PALOMIDES.

It seems as though the sky itself were flowing towards us. . .

ALLADINE.

It is full of motionless flowers. . .

PALOMIDES.

Full of strange and motionless flowers. . . See, there is one out yonder, larger than all the others, that shoots out its petals beneath them. . . One can almost hear the rhythmic beat of its life. . . And the water, if water it be, seems bluer, more beautiful, purer than all the waters of earth. . .

ALLADINE.

I am afraid to look any longer. . .

ALLADINE AND   ACT IV.

PALOMIDES.

See how the light now shines over all. . . The light dare no longer waver: and in the vestibule of heaven do we kiss one another. . . Look at the jewels in the roof: they are drunk with life, they seem to smile on us; look at the myriad roses, of deep glowing blue, that twine themselves all round the pillars. . .

ALLADINE.

Oh! . . . I heard! . . .

PALOMIDES.

What?

ALLADINE.

I heard someone striking the rocks. . .

PALOMIDES.

No, no; it is only the golden gates of an unknown heaven that are flung open wide in our soul, and sing as they turn on their hinges! . . .

ALLADINE.

Listen . . . again, again! . . .

PALOMIDES (*with a sudden change of voice*).

Yes; it is out yonder . . . beneath the vault that is bluest of all. . .

ALLADINE.

They are coming to . . .

PALOMIDES.

I hear the iron striking the rock. . . They walled up the door, perhaps, or are unable to open it. . .

ACT IV.   **PALOMIDES**

The axes scrunch on the stone. . . His soul has whispered to him that we were happy. . .

[*A silence; then a stone falls away from the extreme end of the roof, and a ray of daylight breaks into the cavern.*

ALLADINE.

Oh ! . . .

PALOMIDES.

This light is different. . .

[*They stand there, motionless, anxiously watching stone after stone as it slides slowly away and falls to the ground, beneath a light that can scarcely be borne; a light that streams into the cavern with ever more resistless abundance, revealing little by little the wretchedness of the grotto that had seemed so marvellous to them; the miraculous lake becomes dull and sinister; the light fades out of the stones in the rocks, and the ardent roses are seen to be nothing but fungus and decaying matter. At last a whole side of the rock falls bodily into the grotto. The sun streams in, overwhelming all. Shouts and cries are heard from without. Alladine and Palomides draw back.*

PALOMIDES.

Where are we?

ALLADINE (*embracing him sadly*).

And yet do I love you, Palomides. . .

PALOMIDES.

I love you too, my Alladine. . .

51

ALLADINE.
They are coming. . .

    PALOMIDES (*looking behind him as they retreat still further*).

Take care. . .
ALLADINE.
No, no, we need no longer take care. . .

    PALOMIDES (*looking at her*).

Alladine ? . . .
ALLADINE.
Yes.

    [*They retreat further and further before the invasion of light or danger, until at length they lose their footing; they fall, and disappear behind the rock that overhangs the subterranean water, now all enwrapped in gloom. There is a moment's silence; then Astolaine and the sisters of Palomides enter the grotto.*

ASTOLAINE.
Where are they ?

    ONE OF PALOMIDES' SISTERS.

Palomides!
ASTOLAINE.
Alladine, Alladine!

    ANOTHER SISTER.

Palomides! We are here!

    A THIRD SISTER.

Fear nothing; we are alone!

ACT IV. **PALOMIDES**

ASTOLAINE.

Come to us; we are here to save you!

A FOURTH SISTER.

Ablamore has fled...

A FIFTH SISTER.

He is no longer in the palace...

A SIXTH SISTER.

They do not answer...

ASTOLAINE.

I heard a movement in the water—this way, this way!
[*They rush to the rock that hangs over the subterranean water.*

ONE OF THE SISTERS.

There they are!

ANOTHER SISTER.

Yes, yes, at the bottom of the black water... They are lying in each other's arms...

A THIRD SISTER.

They are dead!

A FOURTH SISTER.

No, no, they live, they live... Look...

THE OTHER SISTERS.

Help! Help! Call for help!

ASTOLAINE.

They make no effort to save themselves...

ACT V

Scene

A corridor. It is so long that the last arches seem to be lost in a kind of inner horizon. Innumerable doors, all of them closed, are seen on both sides of the corridor; the sisters of Palomides stand before one of these, over which they seem to keep guard. A little further, on the opposite side, Astolaine stands, speaking to the doctor, in front of a door which is also closed

ASTOLAINE (*to the doctor*).

Hitherto nothing had happened, in this palace, where all seemed to have been steeped in slumber since the death of my sisters; then a strange unreasoning restlessness seized hold of my poor father—he began to chafe under this tranquillity that yet would seem to be the least dangerous form of happiness. Some time ago—his reason must have already been shaken—he climbed to the top of the tower, and stretched both his arms out, timidly, towards mountain and sea; and said to me—with a diffident smile, for he saw that I looked incredulous—that he was summoning to us the events that too long had remained concealed in the horizon. Alas, the events have come: more quickly, more numerous too, than he had expected; and it has needed a few days only for them to dethrone him and reign in his stead. He was the first of their victims. He fled to the meadows, singing and weeping, the night he had caused little Alladine and ill-fated Palomides to be entombed in the grotto. And since then no

ACT V.   PALOMIDES

one has seen him. I have sent men in search of him all over the country, and even on to the sea. They have found not a trace of him. But at least I had hoped to save those on whom he had unconsciously brought this suffering, he who always had been the tenderest of men and the best of fathers; but here too I fear I have come too late. I know nothing of what took place. So far they have said not a word. It appears that they thought, when they heard the iron crushing the stone and the light streamed into the cave, that my father regretted the respite he had accorded and that they who approached brought death. Or it may be that they lost their footing as they retreated along the rock which hangs over the lake, and fell in by accident. But the water there is not deep; and we had no difficulty in saving them. At present it is you, and you only, on whom all depends. . . .

[*The sisters of Palomides have drawn near to them.*

The Doctor.

They are suffering both from the same disease, and it is one that I know not.—But I have little hope. It may be that the chill of that underground water has seized hold of them; or the water itself perhaps may be poisonous. The decomposed body of Alladine's lamb has been found there.—I will come again this evening. In the meantime, they need silence. . . Life has ebbed very low in their heart. . . Do not enter their rooms, or speak to them; for in their present state the least word may be fatal. . . They must try to forget one another. . .   [*He goes.*

One of Palomides' Sisters.

I can see that he is going to die. . .

Astolaine.

No, no . . . do not weep . . . at his age death does not come so quickly. . .

Another Sister.

Why was your father so angry with our poor brother? He had no cause. . .

The Third Sister.

I believe your father must have loved Alladine. . .

Astolaine.

Do not speak of him thus. . . He thought I was unhappy. He imagined he was doing right, and did wrong without knowing it. . . That happens often to us all. . . I remember now. . . One night I was asleep; and wept in my dream. . . We have so little courage when we dream. . . I awoke; he was standing by my bedside, looking at me. . . And he misunderstood, perhaps . . .

The Fourth Sister (*hurrying towards them*).

I heard Alladine move in her room. . .

Astolaine.

Go to the door; listen—it is perhaps only the nurse. . .

The Fifth Sister.

No, no; I can hear the nurse's footsteps. . . This noise is different. . .

ACT V.   **PALOMIDES**

          The Sixth Sister.

I believe Palomides has moved too. . . . I seemed to hear a voice that was striving to speak. . .

The Voice of Alladine (*very feebly, from within the room*).
Palomides! . . .

          One of the Sisters.

She is calling to him! . . .

          Astolaine.

We must take care! . . . Go, stand in front of the door, so that Palomides may not hear. . .

          The Voice of Alladine.

Palomides! . . .

          Astolaine.

O God, O God, silence that voice! If Palomides hears it, he will die! . . .

The Voice of Palomides (*very feebly, from within another room*).
Alladine! . . .

          One of the Sisters.

He is answering! . . .

          Astolaine.

Do three of you stay here; the rest of us will go to the other door. Come, we must hasten—we will surround them, try to protect them. . . Lie right against the panels—perhaps they will not hear. . .

          One of the Sisters.

I will go in to Alladine. . .

The Second Sister.

Yes, yes; prevent her from calling again. . .

The Third Sister.

It is she who has caused all this sorrow. . .

Astolaine.

You shall not go in; or if you do then will I go to Palomides. She had the same right to live as the rest of us, and she has done nothing more. . . But to be unable to stifle these death-dealing words as they pass by us! . . . We can do nothing, my sisters, my poor sisters, we can do nothing; and the hand cannot stay the soul! . . .

The Voice of Alladine.

Palomides—is that you?

The Voice of Palomides.

Where are you, Alladine?

The Voice of Alladine.

Is it you that I hear moaning, far away from me?

The Voice of Palomides.

Is it you that I have heard calling me?—I cannot see you. . .

The Voice of Alladine.

Your voice seems to have lost all hope. . .

The Voice of Palomides.

Yours seems already to have passed through death. . .

ACT V.   **PALOMIDES**

          The Voice of Alladine.
Your voice scarcely reaches my room. . .

          The Voice of Palomides.
Nor does yours sound to me as it used to sound. . .

          The Voice of Alladine.
I had pity on you! . . .

          The Voice of Palomides.
They have parted us, but I always shall love you. . .

          The Voice of Alladine.
I had pity on you . . . are you suffering still?

          The Voice of Palomides.
I suffer no more, but I want to see you. . .

          The Voice of Alladine.
Never again shall we see one another, for the doors are all closed. . .

          The Voice of Palomides.
There is that in your voice that tells me you love me no longer. . .

          The Voice of Alladine.
Yes, yes, I love you still, but now all is sorrow. . .

          The Voice of Palomides.
You are turning away. . . I scarcely can hear you. . .

          The Voice of Alladine.
We seem to be hundreds of miles from each other. . .

The Voice of Palomides.

I have tried to rise, but my soul is too heavy. . .

The Voice of Alladine.

I have tried, too, but my head fell back. . .

The Voice of Palomides.

As I listen I seem to hear your tears fall. . .

The Voice of Alladine.

No; for a long time I wept; but now these are no longer tears. . .

The Voice of Palomides.

You are thinking of something that you will not tell me. . .

The Voice of Alladine.

They were not jewels. . .

The Voice of Palomides.

And the flowers were not real. . .

One of Palomides' Sisters.

They are delirious. . .

Astolaine.

No, no; they are well aware of what they are saying. . .

The Voice of Alladine.

It was the light that had no pity. . .

ACT V. **PALOMIDES**

> THE VOICE OF PALOMIDES.

Whither go you, Alladine? You seem to be further and further away from me...

> THE VOICE OF ALLADINE.

I no longer regret the rays of the sun...

> THE VOICE OF PALOMIDES.

Yes, yes, we shall again behold the trees and the flowers!...

> THE VOICE OF ALLADINE.

I have lost the desire to live...

> *[A silence; then more and more feebly,*

> THE VOICE OF PALOMIDES.

Alladine!...

> THE VOICE OF ALLADINE.

Palomides!...

> THE VOICE OF PALOMIDES.

Alla—dine...

> *[A silence. Astolaine and the sisters of Palomides are listening in intense anguish. Then the nurse throws open the door of Palomides' room from within, appears on the threshold, and beckons to them; they all follow her into the room and close the door. Once more there is silence. Then the door of Alladine's room opens; the other nurse comes out and looks about her in the corridor; seeing no one she goes back into the room, leaving the door wide open.*

INTERIOR

TRANSLATED BY WILLIAM ARCHER

CHARACTERS

IN THE GARDEN—

    THE OLD MAN.

    THE STRANGER.

    MARTHA } *Granddaughters of the Old Man.*
    MARY

    A PEASANT.

    THE CROWD.

IN THE HOUSE—

    THE FATHER
    THE MOTHER
    THE TWO DAUGHTERS } *Silent personages.*
    THE CHILD

INTERIOR

An old garden planted with willows. At the back, a house, with three of the ground-floor windows lighted up. Through them a family is pretty distinctly visible, gathered for the evening round the lamp. The Father is seated at the chimney-corner. The Mother, resting one elbow on the table, is gazing into vacancy. Two young girls, dressed in white, sit at their embroidery, dreaming and smiling in the tranquillity of the room. A child is asleep, his head resting on his mother's left arm. When one of them rises, walks, or makes a gesture, the movements appear grave, slow, apart, and as though spiritualised by the distance, the light, and the transparent film of the window-panes.

The OLD MAN *and the* STRANGER *enter the garden cautiously.*

THE OLD MAN.

Here we are in the part of the garden that lies behind the house. They never come here. The doors are on the other side. They are closed and the shutters shut. But there are no shutters on this side of the house, and I saw the light. . . . Yes, they are still sitting up in the lamplight. It is well that they have not heard us; the mother or the girls would perhaps have come out, and then what should we have done?

INTERIOR

The Stranger.

What are we going to do?

The Old Man.

I want first to see if they are all in the room. Yes, I see the father seated at the chimney corner. He is doing nothing, his hands resting on his knees. The mother is leaning her elbow on the table. . . .

The Stranger.

She is looking at us.

The Old Man.

No, she is looking at nothing; her eyes are fixed. She cannot see us; we are in the shadow of the great trees. But do not go any nearer. . . . There, too, are the dead girl's two sisters; they are embroidering slowly. And the little child has fallen asleep. It is nine on the clock in the corner. . . . They divine no evil, and they do not speak.

The Stranger.

If we were to attract the father's attention, and make some sign to him? He has turned his head this way. Shall I knock at one of the windows? One of them will have to hear of it before the others. . . .

The Old Man.

I do not know which to choose. . . . We must be very careful. The father is old and ailing—the mother

INTERIOR

too—and the sisters are too young. . . . And they all loved her as they will never love again. I have never seen a happier household. . . . No, no! do not go up to the window; that would be the worst thing we could do. It is better that we should tell them of it as simply as we can, as though it were a commonplace occurrence; and we must not appear too sad, else they will feel that their sorrow must exceed ours, and they will not know what to do. . . . Let us go round to the other side of the garden. We will knock at the door, and go in as if nothing had happened. I will go in first: they will not be surprised to see me; I sometimes look in of an evening, to bring them some flowers or fruit, and to pass an hour or two with them.

The Stranger.

Why do you want me to go with you? Go alone; I will wait until you call me. They have never seen me— I am only a passer-by, a stranger. . . .

The Old Man.

It is better that I should not be alone. A misfortune announced by a single voice seems more definite and crushing. I thought of that as I came along . . . If I go in alone, I shall have to speak at the very first moment; they will know all in a few words; I shall have nothing more to say; and I dread the silence which follows the last words that tell of a misfortune. It is then that the heart is torn. If we enter together, I shall go roundabout to work; I shall tell them, for example: "They found

INTERIOR

her thus, or thus . . . She was floating on the stream, and her hands were clasped . . ."

THE STRANGER.

Her hands were not clasped; her arms were floating at her sides.

THE OLD MAN.

You see, in spite of ourselves we begin to talk—and the misfortune is shrouded in its details. Otherwise, if I go in alone, I know them well enough to be sure that the very first words would produce a terrible effect, and God knows what would happen. But if we speak to them in turns, they will listen to us, and will forget to look the evil tidings in the face. Do not forget that the mother will be there, and that her life hangs by a thread. . . . It is well that the first wave of sorrow should waste its strength in unnecessary words. It is wisest to let people gather round the unfortunate and talk as they will. Even the most indifferent carry off, without knowing it, some portion of the sorrow. It is dispersed without effort and without noise, like air or light. . . .

THE STRANGER.

Your clothes are soaked and are dripping on the flagstones.

THE OLD MAN.

It is only the skirt of my mantle that has trailed a little in the water. You seem to be cold. Your coat is all muddy . . . I did not notice it on the way, it was so dark.

INTERIOR

The Stranger.

I went into the water up to my waist.

The Old Man.

Had you found her long when I came up?

The Stranger.

Only a few moments. I was going towards the village; it was already late, and the dusk was falling on the river bank. I was walking along with my eyes fixed on the river, because it was lighter than the road, when I saw something strange close by a tuft of reeds. . . . I drew nearer, and I saw her hair, which had floated up almost into a circle round her head, and was swaying hither and thither with the current . . .
[*In the room, the two young girls turn their heads towards the window.*

The Old Man.

Did you see her two sisters' hair trembling on their shoulders?

The Stranger.

They turned their heads in our direction—they simply turned their heads. Perhaps I was speaking too loudly. (*The two girls resume their former position.*) They have turned away again already. . . . I went into the water up to my waist, and then I managed to grasp her hand and easily drew her to the bank. She was as beautiful as her sisters. . . .

INTERIOR

The Old Man.

I think she was more beautiful. . . . I do not know why I have lost all my courage. . . .

The Stranger.

What courage do you mean? We did all that man could do. She had been dead for more than a hour.

The Old Man.

She was living this morning! I met her coming out of the church. She told me that she was going away; she was going to see her grandmother on the other side of the river in which you found her. She did not know when I should see her again. . . . She seemed to be on the point of asking me something; then I suppose she did not dare, and she left me abruptly. But now that I think of it—and I noticed nothing at the time!—she smiled as people smile who want to be silent, or who fear that they will not be understood. . . . Even hope seemed like a pain to her; her eyes were veiled, and she scarcely looked at me.

The Stranger.

Some peasants told me that they saw her wandering all the afternoon upon the bank. They thought she was looking for flowers. . . . It is possible that her death . . . .

The Old Man.

No one can tell. . . . What can anyone know? She was perhaps one of those who shrink from speech, and everyone bears in his breast more than one reason for ceasing to live. You cannot see into

INTERIOR

the soul as you see into that room. They are all like that—they say nothing but trivial things, and no one dreams that there is aught amiss. You live for months by the side of one who is no longer of this world, and whose soul cannot stoop to it; you answer her unthinkingly; and you see what happens. They look like lifeless puppets, and all the time so many things are passing in their souls. They do not themselves know what they are. She might have lived as the others live. She might have said to the day of her death: "Sir, or Madam, it will rain this morning," or, "We are going to lunch; we shall be thirteen at table," or "The fruit is not yet ripe." They speak smilingly of the flowers that have fallen, and they weep in the darkness. An angel from heaven would not see what ought to be seen; and men understand nothing until after all is over. . . . Yesterday evening she was there, sitting in the lamplight like her sisters; and you would not see them now as they ought to be seen if this had not happened. . . . I seem to see her for the first time. . . . Something new must come into our ordinary life before we can understand it. They are at your side day and night; and you do not really see them until the moment when they depart for ever. And yet, what a strange little soul she must have had—what a poor little, artless, unfathomable soul she must have had—to have said what she must have said, and done what she must have done!

THE STRANGER.

See, they are smiling in the silence of the room . . . .

THE OLD MAN.

They are not at all anxious—they did not expect her this evening.

THE STRANGER.

They sit motionless and smiling. But see, the father puts his finger to his lips . . . .

THE OLD MAN.

He points to the child asleep on its mother's breast . . . .

THE STRANGER.

She dares not raise her head for fear of disturbing it . . . .

THE OLD MAN.

They are not sewing any more. There is a dead silence . . . .

THE STRANGER.

They have let fall their skein of white silk . . . .

THE OLD MAN.

They are looking at the child . . . .

THE STRANGER.

They do not know that others are looking at them . . . .

THE OLD MAN.

We, too, are watched . . . .

THE STRANGER.

They have raised their eyes . . . .

THE OLD MAN.

And yet they can see nothing . . . .

INTERIOR

The Stranger.

They seem to be happy, and yet there is something—I cannot tell what . . . .

The Old Man.

They think themselves beyond the reach of danger. They have closed the doors, and the windows are barred with iron. They have strengthened the walls of the old house; they have shot the bolts of the three oaken doors. They have foreseen everything that can be foreseen . . . .

The Stranger.

Sooner or later we must tell them. Someone might come and blurt it out abruptly. There was a crowd of peasants in the meadow where we left the dead girl—if one of them were to come and knock at the door . . . .

The Old Man.

Martha and Mary are watching the little body. The peasants were going to make a litter of branches; and I told my eldest granddaughter to hurry on and let us know the moment they made a start. Let us wait till she comes; she will go with me. . . . . I wish we had not been able to watch them in this way. I thought there was nothing to do but to knock at the door, to enter quite simply, and to tell all in a few phrases. . . . But I have watched them too long, living in the lamplight . . . .

Enter Mary.

Mary.

They are coming, grandfather.

INTERIOR

THE OLD MAN.

Is that you? Where are they?

MARY.

They are at the foot of the last slope.

THE OLD MAN.

They are coming silently.

MARY.

I told them to pray in a low voice. Martha is with them.

THE OLD MAN.

Are there many of them?

MARY.

The whole village is around the bier. They had brought lanterns; I bade them put them out.

THE OLD MAN.

What way are they coming?

MARY.

They are coming by the little paths. They are moving slowly.

THE OLD MAN.

It is time . . . .

MARY.

Have you told them, grandfather?

THE OLD MAN.

You can see that we have told them nothing. There they are, still sitting in the lamplight. Look, my child, look: you will see what life is . . . .

INTERIOR

Mary.
Oh! how peaceful they seem! I feel as though I were seeing them in a dream.

The Stranger.
Look there—I saw the two sisters give a start.

The Old Man.
They are rising . . . .

The Stranger.
I believe they are coming to the windows.

[*At this moment one of the two sisters comes up to the first window, the other to the third; and resting their hands against the panes they stand gazing into the darkness.*

The Old Man.
No one comes to the middle window.

Mary.
They are looking out; they are listening . . . .

The Old Man.
The elder is smiling at what she does not see.

The Stranger.
The eyes of the second are full of fear.

The Old Man.
Take care: who knows how far the soul may extend around the body . . . .

[*A long silence. Mary nestles close to the old man's breast and kisses him.*

INTERIOR

Mary.
Grandfather!

The Old Man.
Do not weep, my child; our turn will come. [*A pause.*

The Stranger.
They are looking long . . . .

The Old Man.
Poor things, they would see nothing though they looked for a hundred thousand years—the night is too dark. They are looking this way; and it is from the other side that misfortune is coming.

The Stranger.
It is well that they are looking this way. Something, I do not know what, is approaching by way of the meadows.

Mary.
I think it is the crowd; they are too far off for us to see clearly.

The Stranger.
They are following the windings of the path—there they come in sight again on that moonlit slope.

Mary.
Oh! how many they seem to be. Even when I left, people were coming up from the outskirts of the town. They are taking a very roundabout way . . . .

The Old Man.
They will arrive at last, none the less. I see them, too—

INTERIOR

they are crossing the meadows—they look so small that one can scarcely distinguish them among the herbage. You might think them children playing in the moonlight; if the girls saw them they would not understand. Turn their backs to it as they may, misfortune is approaching step by step, and has been looming larger for more than two hours past. They cannot bid it stay; and those who are bringing it are powerless to stop it. It has mastered them, too, and they must needs serve it. It knows its goal, and it takes its course. It is unwearying, and it has but one idea. They have to lend it their strength. They are sad, but they draw nearer. Their hearts are full of pity, but they must advance . . . .

MARY.

The elder has ceased to smile, grandfather.

THE STRANGER.

They are leaving the windows . . . .

MARY.

They are kissing their mother . . . .

THE STRANGER.

The elder is stroking the child's curls without wakening it.

MARY.

Ah! the father wants them to kiss him, too . . . .

THE STRANGER.

Now there is silence . . . .

INTERIOR

MARY.

They have returned to their mother's side.

THE STRANGER.

And the father keeps his eyes fixed on the great pendulum of the clock. . . .

MARY.

They seem to be praying without knowing what they do . . . .

THE STRANGER.

They seem to be listening to their own souls . . . .

[*A pause.*

MARY.

Grandfather, do not tell them this evening!

THE OLD MAN.

You see, you are losing courage, too. I knew you ought not to look at them. I am nearly eighty-three years old, and this is the first time that the reality of life has come home to me. I do not know why all they do appears to me so strange and solemn. There they sit awaiting the night, simply, under their lamp, as we should under our own; and yet I seem to see them from the altitude of another world, because I know a little fact which as yet they do not know. . . . Is it so, my children? Tell me, why are you, too, pale? Perhaps there is something else that we cannot put in words, and that makes us weep? I did not know that there was anything so sad in life, or that it could strike such terror to those who look on at it. And even if nothing had happened, it would frighten me to see them sit there so peacefully.

INTERIOR

They have too much confidence in this world. There they sit, separated from the enemy by only a few poor panes of glass. They think that nothing will happen because they have closed their doors, and they do not know that it is in the soul that things always happen, and that the world does not end at their house-door. They are so secure of their little life, and do not dream that so many others know more of it than they, and that I, poor old man, at two steps from their door, hold all their little happiness, like a wounded bird, in the hollow of my old hands, and dare not open them . . . .

MARY.

Have pity on them, grandfather . . . .

THE OLD MAN.

We have pity on them, my child, but no one has pity on us.

MARY.

Tell them to-morrow, grandfather; tell them when it is light, then they will not be so sad.

THE OLD MAN.

Perhaps you are right, my child. . . . It would be better to leave all this in the night. And the daylight is sweet to sorrow. . . . But what would they say to us to-morrow? Misfortune makes people jealous: those upon whom it has fallen want to know of it before strangers—they do not like to leave it in unknown hands. We should seem to have robbed them of something.

INTERIOR

The Stranger.

Besides, it is too late now; already I can hear the murmur of prayers.

Mary.

They are here—they are passing behind the hedges.

Enter Martha.

Martha.

Here I am. I have guided them hither—I told them to wait in the road. (*Cries of children are heard.*) Ah! the children are still crying. I forbade them to come, but they want to see, too, and the mothers would not obey me. I will go and tell them—no, they have stopped crying. Is everything ready? I have brought the little ring that was found upon her. I have some fruit, too, for the child. I laid her to rest myself upon the bier. She looks as though she were sleeping. I had a great deal of trouble with her hair—I could not arrange it properly. I made them gather marguerites—it is a pity there were no other flowers. What are you doing here? Why are you not with them? (*She looks in at the windows.*) They are not weeping! They—you have not told them!

The Old Man.

Martha, Martha, there is too much life in your soul; you cannot understand . . . .

Martha.

Why should I not understand? (*After a silence, and in*

INTERIOR

a tone of grave reproach) You ought not to have done that, grandfather . . . .

THE OLD MAN.
Martha, you do not know . . . .

MARTHA.
I will go and tell them.

THE OLD MAN.
Remain here, my child, and look for a moment.

MARTHA.
Oh, how I pity them! They must wait no longer . . .

THE OLD MAN.
Why not?

MARTHA.
I do not know, but it is not possible!

THE OLD MAN.
Come here, my child . . . .

MARTHA.
How patient they are!

THE OLD MAN.
Come here, my child . . .

MARTHA (*turning*).
Where are you, grandfather? I am so unhappy, I cannot see you any more. I do not myself know now what to do . . . .

INTERIOR

The Old Man.

Do not look any more; until they know all . . . .

Martha.

I want to go with you . . . .

The Old Man.

No, Martha, stay here. Sit beside your sister on this old stone bench against the wall of the house, and do not look. You are too young, you would never be able to forget it. You cannot know what a face looks like at the moment when Death is passing into its eyes. Perhaps they will cry out, too. . . . Do not turn round. Perhaps there will be no sound at all. Above all things, if there is no sound, be sure you do not turn and look. One can never foresee the course that sorrow will take. A few little sobs wrung from the depths, and generally that is all. I do not know myself what I shall do when I hear them—they do not belong to this life. Kiss me, my child, before I go.

[*The murmur of prayers has gradually drawn nearer. A portion of the crowd forces its way into the garden. There is a sound of deadened footfalls and of whispering.*

The Stranger (*to the crowd*).

Stop here—do not go near the window. Where is she?

A Peasant.

Who?

The Stranger.

The others—the bearers.

INTERIOR

A Peasant.
They are coming by the avenue that leads up to the door.
[The Old Man goes out. Martha and Mary have seated themselves on the bench, their backs to the windows. Low murmurings are heard among the crowd.

The Stranger.
Hush! Do not speak.
[In the room the taller of the two sisters rises, goes to the door, and shoots the bolts.

Martha.
She is opening the door?

The Stranger.
On the contrary, she is fastening it. *[A pause.*

Martha.
Grandfather has not come in?

The Stranger.
No. She takes her seat again at her mother's side. The others do not move, and the child is still sleeping. *[A pause.*

Martha.
My little sister, give me your hands.

Mary.
Martha! *[They embrace and kiss each other.*

The Stranger.
He must have knocked—they have all raised their heads at the same time—they are looking at each other.

INTERIOR

MARTHA.

Oh! oh! my poor little sister! I can scarcely help crying out, too.
  [*She smothers her sobs on her sister's shoulder.*

THE STRANGER.

He must have knocked again. The father is looking at the clock. He rises....

MARTHA.

Sister, sister, I must go in too—they cannot be left alone.

MARY.

Martha, Martha! [*She holds her back.*

THE STRANGER.

The father is at the door—he is drawing the bolts—he is opening it cautiously.

MARTHA.

Oh!—you do not see the ....

THE STRANGER.

What?

MARTHA.

The bearers ....

THE STRANGER.

He has only opened it a very little. I see nothing but a corner of the lawn and the fountain. He keeps his hand on the door—He takes a step back—he seems to be saying, "Ah, it is you!" He raises his arms.

INTERIOR

He carefully closes the door again. Your grandfather has entered the room . . . .

[*The crowd has come up to the window. Martha and Mary half rise from their seat, then rise altogether and follow the rest towards the windows, pressing close to each other. The Old Man is seen advancing into the room. The two Sisters rise; the Mother also rises, and carefully settles the Child in the armchair which she has left, so that from outside the little one can be seen sleeping, his head a little bent forward, in the middle of the room. The Mother advances to meet the Old Man, and holds out her hand to him, but draws it back again before he has had time to take it. One of the girls wants to take off the visitor's mantle, and the other pushes forward an armchair for him. But the Old Man makes a little gesture of refusal. The Father smiles with an air of astonishment. The Old Man looks towards the windows.*

THE STRANGER.

He dares not tell them. He is looking towards us.

[*Murmurs in the crowd.*

THE STRANGER.

Hush!

[*The Old Man, seeing faces at the windows, quickly averts his eyes. As one of the girls is still offering him the armchair, he at last sits down and passes his right hand several times over his forehead.*

INTERIOR

The Stranger.

He is sitting down . . . .
> [*The others who are in the room also sit down, while the Father seems to be speaking volubly. At last the Old Man opens his mouth, and the sound of his voice seems to arouse their attention. But the Father interrupts him. The Old Man begins to speak again, and little by little the others grow tense with apprehension. All of a sudden the Mother starts and rises.*

Martha.

Oh! the mother begins to understand!
> [*She turns away and hides her face in her hands. Renewed murmurs among the crowd. They elbow each other. Children cry to be lifted up, so that they may see too. Most of the mothers do as they wish.*

The Stranger.

Hush! he has not told them yet . . . .
> [*The Mother is seen to be questioning the Old Man with anxiety. He says a few more words; then, suddenly, all the others rise, too, and seem to question him. Then he slowly makes an affirmative movement of his head.*

The Stranger.

He has told them—he has told them all at once!

Voices in the Crowd.

He has told them! he has told them!

INTERIOR

THE STRANGER.

I can hear nothing . . . .
> [*The Old Man also rises, and, without turning, makes a gesture indicating the door, which is behind him. The Mother, the Father, and the two Daughters rush to this door, which the Father has difficulty in opening. The Old Man tries to prevent the Mother from going out*

VOICES IN THE CROWD.

They are going out! they are going out!
> [*Confusion among the crowd in the garden. All hurry to the other side of the house and disappear, except the Stranger, who remains at the windows. In the room, the folding door is at last thrown wide open; all go out at the same time. Beyond can be seen the starry sky, the lawn and the fountain in the moonlight; while, left alone in the middle of the room, the Child continues to sleep peacefully in the armchair. A pause.*

THE STRANGER.

The child has not awakened!   [*He also goes out.*

THE DEATH OF TINTAGILES

TRANSLATED BY ALFRED SUTRO

CHARACTERS

TINTAGILES.
YGRAINE
BELLANGÈRE } *Sisters of Tintagiles.*
AGLOVALE.
THREE SERVANTS *of the Queen.*

ACT I

SCENE

On the top of a hill overlooking the castle

Enter YGRAINE, *holding* TINTAGILES *by the hand.*

YGRAINE.

Your first night will be sad, Tintagiles. The roar of the sea is already about us; and the trees are moaning. It is late. The moon is sinking behind the poplars that stifle the palace. . . . We are alone, perhaps; but here, one has ever to be on one's guard. They seem to watch lest the smallest happiness come near. I said to myself one day, right down in the depths of my soul—and God himself could scarcely hear;—I said to myself one day that I was feeling almost happy. . . There needed nothing more; and very soon after, our old father died, and our two brothers disappeared, and not a living creature can tell us where they are. I am here all alone, with my poor sister and you, my little Tintagiles; and I have no confidence in the future. . . Come to me; let me take you on my knees. First kiss me; and put your little arms—there—right round my neck . . . perhaps they will not be able to unfasten them. . . Do you remember the time when it was I who carried you in the evening, when the hour had come; and how frightened you were at the shadows of my lamp in the corridors, those long corridors with not a single window? I felt my soul tremble on my lips when I saw you again, suddenly, this morning. . . I thought you were so far away and in safety. . . Who made you come here?

TINTAGILES.

I do not know, little sister.

YGRAINE.

Do you remember what they said?

TINTAGILES.

They said I must go away.

YGRAINE.

But why had you to go away?

TINTAGILES.

Because the Queen wished it.

YGRAINE.

Did they not say why she wished it?—I am sure they must have said many things.

TINTAGILES.

Little sister, I did not hear.

YGRAINE.

When they spoke among themselves, what was it they said?

ACT I. **TINTAGILES**

>TINTAGILES.

Little sister, they dropped their voices when they spoke.

>YGRAINE.

All the time?

>TINTAGILES.

All the time, sister Ygraine; except when they looked at me.

>YGRAINE.

Did they say nothing about the Queen?

>TINTAGILES.

They said, sister Ygraine, that no one ever saw her.

>YGRAINE.

And the people who were with you on the ship, did they say nothing?

>TINTAGILES.

They gave all their time to the wind and the sails, sister Ygraine.

>YGRAINE.

Ah!... That does not surprise me, my child...

>TINTAGILES.

They left me all alone, little sister.

>YGRAINE.

Listen to me, Tintagiles; I will tell you what I know...

>TINTAGILES.

What do you know, sister Ygraine?

YGRAINE.

Very little, my child. . / My sister and I have gone on living here ever since we were born, not daring to understand the things that happened.) . . I have lived a long time in this island, and I might as well have been blind; yet it all seemed natural to me. . . A bird that flew, a leaf that trembled, a rose that opened . . . these were events to me. Such silence has always reigned here that a ripe fruit falling in the park would draw faces to the window. . . And no one seemed to have any suspicion . . . but one night I learned that there must be something besides. . . I wished to escape and I could not. . / Have you understood what I am telling you?

TINTAGILES.

Yes, yes, little sister; I can understand anything. . .

YGRAINE.

Then let us not talk any more of these things . . . one does not know. . . Do you see, behind the dead trees which poison the horizon, do you see the castle, there, right down in the valley?

TINTAGILES.

I see something very black—is that the castle, sister Ygraine?

YGRAINE.

Yes, it is very black. . . It lies far down amid a mass of gloomy shadows. . . It is there that we have to live. . . . They might have built it on the top of the great mountains that surround it. . . The mountains are

ACT I. **TINTAGILES**

blue in the day-time... One could have breathed. One could have looked down on the sea and on the plains beyond the cliffs... But they preferred to build it deep down in the valley; too low even for the air to come... It is falling in ruins, and no one troubles... The walls are crumbling: it might be fading away in the gloom... There is only one tower which time does not touch... It is enormous: and its shadow is always on the house.

TINTAGILES.

They are lighting something, sister Ygraine... See, see, the great red windows!...

YGRAINE.

They are the windows of the tower, Tintagiles; they are the only ones in which you will ever see light; it is there that the Queen has her throne.

TINTAGILES.

Shall I not see the Queen?

YGRAINE.

No one can see her.

TINTAGILES.

Why can no one see her?

YGRAINE.

Come closer, Tintagiles... Not even a bird or a blade of grass must hear us.

TINTAGILES.

There is no grass, little sister... (*a moment's silence*). What does the Queen do?

YGRAINE.

That no one knows, my child. She is never seen. . . She lives there, all alone in the tower; and those who wait on her do not go out by daylight. . . She is very old; she is the mother of our mother, and she wishes to reign alone. . . She is suspicious and jealous, and they say she is mad. . . She is afraid lest some one should raise himself to her place, and it is probably because of this fear of hers that you have been brought hither. . . Her orders are carried out: but no one knows how. . . She never leaves the tower, and all the gates are closed night and day. . . I have never seen her, but it seems others have, long ago, when she was young. . .

TINTAGILES.

Is she very ugly, sister Ygraine?

YGRAINE.

They say she is not beautiful, and that her form is strange. . . . But those who have seen her dare not speak of her. . . And who knows whether they have seen her? . . . She has a power which we do not understand, and we live here with a terrible weight on our soul. . . You must not be unduly frightened, or have bad dreams; we will watch over you, little Tintagiles, and no harm can come to you; but do not stray far from me, or your sister Bellangère, or our old master Aglovale.

TINTAGILES.

Aglovale, too, sister Ygraine?

ACT I.   **TINTAGILES**

YGRAINE.

Aglovale too . . . he loves us . . .

TINTAGILES.

He is so old, little sister!

YGRAINE.

He is old, but very wise. . . . He is the only friend we have left; and he knows many things. . . . It is strange; she made you come here, and no one was told of it. . . I do not know what is in my heart. . . . I was sorrowful and glad to know that you were far away, beyond the sea. . . . And now . . . I was taken by surprise. . . . I went out this morning to see whether the sun was rising over the mountains; and I saw you on the threshold. . . I knew you at once.

TINTAGILES.

No, no, little sister; it was I who laughed first. . .

YGRAINE.

I could not laugh . . . just then. . . You will understand. . . It is time, Tintagiles, and the wind is becoming black on the sea. . . Kiss me, before getting up; kiss me, harder, again, again. . . You do not know how one loves. . . Give me your little hand. . . I will keep it in mine, and we will go back to the old sick castle.   [*They go out.*

ACT II

SCENE

A room in the castle, in which Aglovale and Ygraine are seated.

Enter BELLANGÈRE.

BELLANGÈRE.

Where is Tintagiles?

YGRAINE.

He is here; do not speak too loud. He is asleep in the other room. He was a little pale, he did not seem well. The journey had tired him—he was a long time on the sea. Or perhaps it is the atmosphere of the castle which has alarmed his little soul. He was crying, and did not know why he cried. I nursed him on my knees; come, look at him. . . He is asleep in our bed. . . He sleeps very gravely, with one hand on his brow, like a little sorrowful king. . .

BELLANGÈRE (*suddenly bursting into tears*).

Sister! Sister! . . . my poor sister! . . .

YGRAINE.

Why are you crying?

BELLANGÈRE.

I dare not tell what I know . . . and I am not sure that I know anything . . . but yet I have heard—that which one could not hear . . .

ACT II. **TINTAGILES**

YGRAINE.

What have you heard?

BELLANGÈRE.

I was passing close to the corridors of the tower . . .

YGRAINE.

Ah! . . .

BELLANGÈRE.

One of the doors was ajar. I pushed it very gently . . . I went in . . .

YGRAINE.

Where?

BELLANGÈRE.

I had never seen. . . There were other corridors lighted with lamps; and then low galleries, which seemed to have no end. . . I knew it was forbidden to go farther. . . I was afraid and was about to turn back, but there was a sound of voices . . . though one could scarcely hear . . .

YGRAINE.

It must have been the servants of the Queen; they live at the foot of the tower . . .

BELLANGÈRE.

I do not know quite what it was. . . . There must have been more than one door between; and the voices came to me like the voice of some one who is being strangled. . . I went as near as I could. . . I am not sure of anything: but I believe they were speaking of a child who had arrived to-day, and of a crown of gold. . . They seemed to be laughing . . .

THE DEATH OF

ACT II.

YGRAINE.

They were laughing?

BELLANGÈRE.

Yes, I think they were laughing . . . unless it was that they were crying, or that it was something I did not understand; for one heard badly, and their voices were low. . . There seemed to be a great many of them moving about in the vault. . . They were speaking of the child that the Queen wished to see. . . They will probably come here this evening . .

YGRAINE.

What? . . . this evening? . . .

BELLANGÈRE.

Yes . . . yes. . . . I think so . . . yes . . .

YGRAINE.

Did they not mention any name?

BELLANGÈRE.

They spoke of a child—a little, little child . . .

YGRAINE.

There is no other child here . . .

BELLANGÈRE.

Just then they raised their voices a little, for one of them had doubted whether the day was come . . .

YGRAINE.

I know what that means, and it will not be the first time that they have left the tower. . . I knew only too well why she made him come . . . but I could not think she would show such haste as this! . . . We shall see . . . there are three of us, and we have time . . .

BELLANGÈRE.

What do you mean to do?

YGRAINE.

I do not know yet what I shall do, but I shall surprise her . . . do you know what that means, you who only can tremble? . . . I will tell you . . .

BELLANGÈRE.

What?

YGRAINE.

She shall not take him without a struggle . . .

BELLANGÈRE.

We are alone, sister Ygraine . . .

YGRAINE.

Ah! it is true we are alone! . . . There is only one thing to be done, and it never fails us! . . . Let us wait on our knees as we did before. . . . Perhaps she will have pity! . . . She allows herself to be moved by tears. . . We must grant her everything she asks; she will smile perhaps; and it is her habit to spare all who kneel. . . All these years she has been there in her enormous tower, devouring those we love, and not a single one has dared strike her in the face. . . She lies on our soul like the stone of a tomb, and no one dares stretch out his arm. . . In the times when there were men here, they too were afraid, and fell upon their faces. . . To-day it is the woman's turn . . . we shall see. . . It is time that some one should dare to rise. . . No one knows on what her power rests, and I will no longer live in the shadow of her tower. . . Go away, if you two can only tremble like this—go away both of you, and leave me still more alone. . . I will wait for her . . .

BELLANGÈRE.

Sister, I do not know what has to be done, but I will wait with you . . .

AGLOVALE.

I too will wait, my daughter. . . My soul has long been ill at ease. . . You will try . . . we have tried more than once . . .

YGRAINE.

You have tried . . . you also?

AGLOVALE.

They have all tried. . . But at the last moment their strength has failed them. . . You too, you shall see. . . . If she were to command me to go up to her this very evening, I would put my two hands together and say nothing; and my weary feet would climb the staircase, without lingering and without hastening, though I know full well that none come down again with eyes unclosed. . . There is no courage left in me against her . . . our hands are helpless, and can touch no one. . . Other hands

ACT II.   **TINTAGILES**

than these are wanted, and all is useless. . . But you are hopeful, and I will assist you. . . Close the doors, my child. . . Awaken Tintagiles; bare your little arms and enfold him within them, and take him on your knees . . . we have no other defence . . .

ACT III

SCENE

The same Room

YGRAINE *and* AGLOVALE.

YGRAINE.

I have been to look at the doors. There are three of them. We will watch the large one. . . The two others are low and heavy. They are never opened. The keys were lost long ago, and the iron bars are sunk into the walls. Help me close this door; it is heavier than the gate of a city. . . It is massive; the lightning itself could not pierce through it. . . you prepared for all that may happen?

AGLOVALE (*seating himself on the threshold*).

I will go seat myself on the steps; my sword upon my knees. . . I do not think this is the first time that I have waited and watched here, my child; and there are moments when one does not understand all that one remembers... I have done all this before, I do not know when... but I have never dared draw my sword... Now, it lies there before me, though my arms no longer have strength; but I intend to try... It is perhaps time that men should defend themselves, even though they do not understand...

[*Bellangère carrying Tintagiles in her arms, comes out of the adjoining room.*]

BELLANGÈRE.

He was awake...

YGRAINE.

He is pale... what ails him?

BELLANGÈRE.

I do not know... he was very silent... He was crying...

YGRAINE.

Tintagiles...

BELLANGÈRE.

He is looking away from you.

YGRAINE.

He does not seem to know me... Tintagiles, where are you?—It is your sister who speaks to you... What are you looking at so fixedly?—Turn round... come, I will play with you....

TINTAGILES.

No... no...

YGRAINE.

You do not want to play?

ACT III.   **TINTAGILES**

####### TINTAGILES.

I cannot stand, sister Ygraine. . .

####### YGRAINE.

You cannot stand? . . . Come, come, what is the matter with you?—Are you suffering any pain? . .

####### TINTAGILES.

Yes. . . .

####### YGRAINE.

Tell me where it is, Tintagiles, and I will cure you. . .

####### TINTAGILES.

I cannot tell, sister Ygraine . . . everywhere. . .

####### YGRAINE.

Come to me, Tintagiles. . . You know that my arms are softer, and I will put them around you, and you will feel better at once. . . Give him to me, Bellangère. . . He shall sit on my knee, and the pain will go. . . . There, you see? . . . Your big sisters are here. . . They are close to you . . . we will defend you, and no evil can come near. . . .

####### TINTAGILES.

It has come, sister Ygraine. . . Why is there no light, sister Ygraine?

####### YGRAINE.

There is a light, my child. . . Do you not see the lamp that hangs from the rafters?

####### TINTAGILES.

Yes, yes. . . It is not large. . . Are there no others?

YGRAINE.

Why should there be others? We can see what we have to see. . .

TINTAGILES.

Ah! . . .

YGRAINE.

Oh! your eyes are deep. . .

TINTAGILES.

So are yours, sister Ygraine. . .

YGRAINE.

I did not notice it this morning. . . I have just seen in your eyes. . . We do not quite know what the soul thinks it sees. . .

TINTAGILES.

I have not seen the soul, sister Ygraine. . . . But why is Aglovale on the threshold?

YGRAINE.

He is resting a little. . . He wanted to kiss you before going to bed . . . he was waiting for you to wake. . . .

TINTAGILES.

What has he on his knees?

YGRAINE.

On his knees? I see nothing on his knees. . .

TINTAGILES.

Yes, yes, there is something. . .

ACT III. **TINTAGILES**

AGLOVALE.

It is nothing, my child. . . I was looking at my old sword; and I scarcely recognise it. . . It has served me many years, but for a long time past I have lost confidence in it, and I think it is going to break. . . Here, just by the hilt, there is a little stain. . . I had noticed that the steel was growing paler, and I asked myself. . . I do not remember what I asked myself. . . My soul is very heavy to-day. . . What is one to do? . . . Men must needs live and await the unforeseen. . . And after that they must still act as if they hoped. . . There are sad evenings when our useless lives taste bitter in our mouths, and we would like to close our eyes. . . It is late, and I am tired. . .

TINTAGILES.

He has wounds, sister Ygraine.

YGRAINE.

Where?

TINTAGILES.

On his forehead and on his hands. . .

AGLOVALE.

Those are very old wounds, from which I suffer no longer, my child. . . The light must be falling on them this evening. . . You had not noticed them before?

TINTAGILES.

He looks sad, sister Ygraine. . .

YGRAINE.

No, no, he is not sad, but very weary. . .

… THE DEATH OF   ACT III.

TINTAGILES.

You too are sad, sister Ygraine. . .

YGRAINE.

Why no, why no; look at me, I am smiling. . .

TINTAGILES.

And my other sister too. . .

YGRAINE.

Oh no, she too is smiling.

TINTAGILES.

No, that is not a smile . . . I know. . .

YGRAINE.

Come, kiss me, and think of something else. . .
                                                [*She kisses him.*

TINTAGILES.

Of what shall I think, sister Ygraine?—Why do you hurt me when you kiss me?

YGRAINE.

Did I hurt you?

TINTAGILES.

Yes. . . I do not know why I hear your heart beat, sister Ygraine. . .

YGRAINE.

Do you hear it beat?

TINTAGILES.

Oh! Oh! it beats as though it wanted to . . .

ACT III.   **TINTAGILES**

YGRAINE.

What?

TINTAGILES.

I do not know, sister Ygraine.

YGRAINE.

It is wrong to be frightened without reason, and to speak in riddles. . . Oh! your eyes are full of tears. . . Why are you unhappy? I hear your heart beating, now . . . people always hear them when they hold one another so close. It is then that the heart speaks and says things that the tongue does not know. . .

TINTAGILES.

I heard nothing before. . .

YGRAINE.

That was because. . . Oh! but your heart! . . . What is the matter? . . . It is bursting! . . .

TINTAGILES (*crying*).

Sister Ygraine! sister Ygraine!

YGRAINE.

What is it?

TINTAGILES.

I have heard. . . They . . . they are coming!

YGRAINE.

Who? Who are coming? . . . What has happened? . . .

THE DEATH OF

TINTAGILES.

The door! the door! They were there! . . .
  [*He falls backwards on to Ygraine's knees.*

YGRAINE.

What is it? . . . He has . . . he has fainted. . .

BELLANGÈRE.

Take care . . . take care . . . He will fall. . .

AGLOVALE (*rising brusquely, his sword in his hand*).
I too can hear . . . there are steps in the corridor.

YGRAINE.

Oh! . . .   [*A moment's silence—they all listen.*

AGLOVALE.

Yes, I hear. . . . There is a crowd of them. . .

YGRAINE.

A crowd . . . a crowd . . . how?

AGLOVALE.

I do not know . . . one hears and one does not hear. . . . They do not move like other creatures, but they come. . . They are touching the door. . .

YGRAINE (*clasping Tintagiles in her arms*).
Tintagiles! . . . Tintagiles! . . .

BELLANGÈRE (*embracing him*).
Let me, too! let me! . . . Tintagiles!

ACT III.   **TINTAGILES**

AGLOVALE.

They are shaking the door . . . listen . . . do not breathe. . . They are whispering. . .

[*A key is heard turning harshly in the lock.*

YGRAINE.

They have the key!

AGLOVALE.

Yes . . . yes. . . . I was sure of it. . . . Wait . . . (*He plants himself, with sword outstretched, on the last step. To the two sisters*) Come! come both! . . .

[*For a moment there is silence. The door opens slowly. Aglovale thrusts his sword wildly through the opening, driving the point between the beams. The sword breaks with a loud report under the silent pressure of the timber, and the pieces of steel roll down the steps with a resounding clang. Ygraine leaps up, carrying in her arms Tintagiles, who has fainted; and she, Bellangère, and Aglovale, putting forth all their strength, try, but in vain, to close the door, which slowly opens wider and wider, although no one can be seen or heard. Only, a cold and calm light penetrates into the room. At this moment Tintagiles, suddenly stretching out his limbs, regains consciousness, sends forth a long cry of deliverance, and embraces his sister—and at this very instant the door, which resists no longer, falls to brusquely under their pressure, which they have not had time to stop.*

YGRAINE.

Tintagiles!   [*They look with amazement at each other.*

THE DEATH OF   ACT III.

AGLOVALE (*waiting at the door*).

I hear nothing now. . .

YGRAINE (*wild with joy*).

Tintagiles! Tintagiles! Look! Look! . . . He is saved! . . . Look at his eyes . . . you can see the blue. . . . He is going to speak. . . They saw we were watching. . . . They did not dare. . . Kiss us! . . . Kiss us, I say! . . . Kiss us! . . . All! all! . . . Down to the depths of our soul! . . .
[*All four, their eyes full of tears, fall into each other's arms.*

ACT IV

SCENE

A corridor in front of the room in which the last Act took place.

Three SERVANTS *of the Queen enter. They are all veiled, and their long black robes flow down to the ground.*

FIRST SERVANT (*listening at the door*).

They are not watching. . .

SECOND SERVANT.

We need not have waited. . .

THIRD SERVANT.

She prefers that it should be done in silence. . .

ACT IV.   **TINTAGILES**

     FIRST SERVANT.
I knew that they must fall asleep. . .
     SECOND SERVANT.
Quick ! . . . open the door. . .
     THIRD SERVANT.
It is time. . .
     FIRST SERVANT.
Wait there . . . I will enter alone.   There is no need for
 three of us. . . .
     SECOND SERVANT.
You are right : he is very small. . .
     THIRD SERVANT.
You must be careful with the elder sister. . .
     SECOND SERVANT.
Remember the Queen does not want them to know. . .
     FIRST SERVANT.
Have no fear, people seldom hear my coming. . .
     SECOND SERVANT.
Go in then ; it is time.
  [*The First Servant opens the door cautiously and
   goes into the room.*
It is close on midnight. . .
     THIRD SERVANT.
Ah ! . . .
  [*A moment's silence.   The First Servant comes out
   of the room.*

THE DEATH OF ACT IV.

SECOND SERVANT.

Where is he?

FIRST SERVANT.

He is asleep between his sisters. His arms are around their necks; and their arms enfold him. . . I cannot do it alone. . .

SECOND SERVANT.

I will help you. . .

THIRD SERVANT.

Yes; do you go together. . . I will keep watch here. . .

FIRST SERVANT.

Be careful; they seem to know. . . They were all three struggling with a bad dream. . .

[*The two Servants go into the room.*

THIRD SERVANT.

People always know; but they do not understand. . .

[*A moment's silence. The First and Second Servants come out of the room again.*

THIRD SERVANT.

Well?

SECOND SERVANT.

You must come too . . . we cannot separate them. . .

FIRST SERVANT.

No sooner do we unclasp their arms than they fall back around the child. . .

SECOND SERVANT.

And the child nestles closer and closer to them. . .

ACT IV. **TINTAGILES**

FIRST SERVANT.

He is lying with his forehead on the elder sister's heart...

SECOND SERVANT.

And his head rises and falls on her bosom...

FIRST SERVANT.

We shall not be able to open his hands...

SECOND SERVANT.

They are plunged deep down into his sisters' hair...

FIRST SERVANT.

He holds one golden curl between his little teeth...

SECOND SERVANT.

We shall have to cut the elder sister's hair.

FIRST SERVANT.

And the other sister's too, you will see...

SECOND SERVANT.

Have you your scissors?

THIRD SERVANT.

Yes...

FIRST SERVANT.

Come quickly; they have begun to move...

SECOND SERVANT.

Their hearts and their eyelids are throbbing together...

FIRST SERVANT.

Yes; I caught a glimpse of the elder girl's blue eyes...

THE DEATH OF   ACT IV.

SECOND SERVANT.

She looked at us but did not see us. . .

FIRST SERVANT.

If one touches one of them, the other two tremble. . .

SECOND SERVANT.

They are trying hard, but they cannot stir. . .

FIRST SERVANT.

The elder sister wishes to scream, but she cannot. . .

SECOND SERVANT.

Come quickly; they seem to know. . .

THIRD SERVANT.

Where is the old man?

FIRST SERVANT.

He is asleep—away from the others. . .

SECOND SERVANT.

He sleeps, his forehead resting on the hilt of his sword. . .

FIRST SERVANT.

He knows of nothing; and he has no dreams. . .

THIRD SERVANT.

Come, come, we must hasten. . .

FIRST SERVANT.

You will find it difficult to separate their limbs. . .

ACT IV.   TINTAGILES

SECOND SERVANT.

They are clutching at each other as though they were drowning.

THIRD SERVANT.

Come, come. . .

[*They go in. The silence is broken only by sighs and low murmurs of suffering, held in thrall by sleep. Then the three Servants emerge very hurriedly from the gloomy room. One of them carries Tintagiles, who is fast asleep, in her arms. From his little hands, twitching in sleep, and his mouth, drawn in agony, a glittering stream of golden tresses, ravished from the heads of his sisters, flows down to the ground. The Servants hurry on. There is perfect silence; but no sooner have they reached the end of the corridor than Tintagiles awakes, and sends forth a cry of supreme distress.*

TINTAGILES (*from the end of the corridor*).

Aah! . . .

[*There is again silence. Then from the adjoining room the two sisters are heard moving about restlessly.*

YGRAINE (*in the room*).

Tintagiles! . . . where is he?

BELLANGÈRE.

He is not here. . .

YGRAINE (*with growing anguish*).

Tintagiles! . . . a lamp, a lamp! . . . Light it! . .

THE DEATH OF ACT V.

BELLANGÈRE.

Yes . . . Yes . . .
 [*Ygraine is seen coming out of the room with the lighted lamp in her hand.*

YGRAINE.

The door is wide open!

The voice of TINTAGILES (*almost inaudible in the distance*).

Sister Ygraine!

YGRAINE.

He calls! . . . He calls! . . . Tintagiles! Tintagiles! . . .
 [*She rushes into the corridor. Bellangère tries to follow, but falls fainting on the threshold.*

ACT V

SCENE

Before a great iron door in a gloomy vault.

Enter YGRAINE, *haggard and dishevelled, with a lamp in her hand.*

YGRAINE (*turning wildly to and fro*).

They have not followed me! . . . Bellangère! . . . Bellangère! . . . Aglovale! . . . Where are they? —They said they loved him and they leave me alone! . . . Tintagiles! . . . Tintagiles! . . . Oh! I remember . . . I have climbed steps without number,

ACT V.   **TINTAGILES**

between great pitiless walls, and my heart bids me live no longer . . . These vaults seem to move . . . (*She supports herself against the pillars.*) I am falling . . . Oh! Oh! my poor life! I can feel it . . . It is trembling on my lips—it wants to depart . . . I know not what I have done . . . I have seen nothing, I have heard nothing . . . Oh, this silence! . . . All along the steps and all along the walls I found these golden curls; and I followed them. I picked them up . . . Oh! oh! they are very pretty! . . . Little childie . . . little childie . . . what was I saying? I remember . . . I do not believe in it . . . When one sleeps . . . All that has no importance and is not possible . . . Of what am I thinking? . . . I do not know . . . One awakes, and then . . . After all—come, after all— I must think this out . . . Some say one thing, some say the other; but the way of the soul is quite different. When the chain is removed, there is much more than one knows. . . I came here with my little lamp. . . It did not go out, in spite of the wind on the staircase . . . And then, what is one to think? There are so many things which are vague . . . There must be people who know them; but why do they not speak? (*She looks around her.*) I have never seen all this before . . . It is difficult to get so far—and it is all forbidden . . . How cold it is . . . And so dark that one is afraid to breathe . . . They say there is poison in these gloomy shadows . . . That door looks very terrible . . . (*She goes up to the door and touches it*). Oh! how cold it is . . . It is of iron . . . solid iron—and there is no lock . . . How can they open it? I see no hinges . . . I suppose it is sunk into the wall . . . This is as far as one can go . . . There are no more steps. (*Suddenly sending forth a terrible shriek*) Ah! . . . more golden hair between the panels! . . . Tintagiles! Tintagiles! . . . I heard the door close just now . . . I remember! I remember! . . . It must be! (*She beats frantically against the door with hands and feet.*) Oh, monster! monster! It is here that I find you! . . . Listen! I blaspheme! I blaspheme and spit on you!

[*Feeble knocks are heard from the other side of the door : then the voice of Tintagiles penetrates very feebly through the iron panels.*

TINTAGILES.

Sister Ygraine, sister Ygraine! . . .

YGRAINE.

Tintagiles! . . . What! . . . what! . . . Tintagiles, is it you? . . .

TINTAGILES.

Quick, open, open! . . . She is here! . . .

YGRAINE.

Oh! oh! . . Who? Tintagiles, my little Tintagiles . . . can you hear me? . . . What is it? . . . What has happened? . . . Tintagiles! . . . Have they hurt you? . . . Where are you? . . . Are you there? . . .

TINTAGILES.

Sister Ygraine, sister Ygraine! . . . Open for me—or I shall die . . .

ACT V.   TINTAGILES

YGRAINE.

I will try—wait, wait . . . I will open it, I will open it. . . .

TINTAGILES.

But you do not understand! . . . Sister Ygraine! . . . There is no time to lose! . . . She tried to hold me back! . . . I struck her, struck her . . . I ran . . . Quick, quick, she is coming!

YGRAINE.

Yes, yes . . . where is she?

TINTAGILES.

I can see nothing . . . but I hear . . . oh, I am afraid, sister Ygraine, I am afraid . . . Quick, quick! . . . Quick, open! . . . for the dear Lord's sake, sister Ygraine! . . .

YGRAINE (*anxiously groping along the door*).

I am sure to find it . . . Wait a little . . . a minute . . . a second. . .

TINTAGILES.

I cannot, sister Ygraine . . . I can feel her breath on me now. . .

YGRAINE.

It is nothing, Tintagiles, my little Tintagiles; do not be frightened . . . if I could only see . . .

TINTAGILES.

Oh, but you can see—I can see your lamp from here . . . It is quite light where you are, sister Ygraine . . . Here I can see nothing. . .

THE DEATH OF ACT V.

YGRAINE.

You see me, Tintagiles? How can you see? There is not a crack in the door . . .

TINTAGILES.

Yes, yes, there is; but it is so small! . . .

YGRAINE.

On which side? Is it here? . . . tell me, tell me . . . or is it over there?

TINTAGILES.

It is here . . . Listen, listen! . . . I am knocking. . .

YGRAINE.

Here?

TINTAGILES.

Higher up . . . But it is so small! . . . A needle could not go through! . . .

YGRAINE.

Do not be afraid, I am here. . .

TINTAGILES.

Oh, I know, sister Ygraine! . . . Pull! pull! You must pull! She is coming! . . . if you could only open a little . . . a very little. . . I am so small!

YGRAINE.

My nails are broken, Tintagiles . . . I have pulled, I have pushed, I have struck with all my might—with all my

ACT V.   **TINTAGILES**

might! (*She strikes again, and tries to shake the massive door.*) Two of my fingers are numbed... Do not cry... It is of iron...

TINTAGILES (*sobbing in despair*).

You have nothing to open with, sister Ygraine?... nothing at all, nothing at all?... I could get through... I am so small, so very small... you know how small I am...

YGRAINE.

I have only my lamp, Tintagiles... There! there! (*She aims repeated blows at the gate with her earthenware lamp, which goes out and breaks, the pieces falling to the ground.*) Oh!... It has all grown dark!... Tintagiles, where are you?... Oh! listen, listen!... Can you not open from the inside?...

TINTAGILES.

No, no; there is nothing... I cannot feel anything at all... I cannot see the light through the crack any more...

YGRAINE.

What is the matter, Tintagiles?... I can scarcely hear you...

TINTAGILES.

Little sister, sister Ygraine... It is too late now...

YGRAINE.

What is it, Tintagiles?... Where are you going?

THE DEATH OF ACT V.

TINTAGILES.

She is here! . . . Oh, I am so weak. Sister Ygraine, sister Ygraine . . . I feel her on me! . . .

YGRAINE.

Whom? . . . whom? . . .

TINTAGILES.

I do not know . . . I cannot see. . . But it is too late now. . . . She . . . she is taking me by the throat. . . . Her hand is at my throat. . . . Oh, oh, sister Ygraine, come to me! . . .

YGRAINE.

Yes, yes. . .

TINTAGILES.

It is so dark. . .

YGRAINE.

Struggle—fight—tear her to pieces! . . . Do not be afraid . . . Wait a moment! . . . I am here . . . Tintagiles? . . . Tintagiles! answer me! . . . Help!!! . . . where are you? . . . I will come to you . . . kiss me . . . through the door . . . here—here.

TINTAGILES (*very feebly*).

Here . . . here . . . sister Ygraine . . .

YGRAINE.

I am putting my kisses on this spot here, do you understand? Again, again!

ACT V. **TINTAGILES**

  TINTAGILES (*more and more feebly*).

Mine too—here . . . sister Ygraine! Sister Ygraine! . . . Oh!
 [*The fall of a little body is heard behind the iron door.*

   YGRAINE.

Tintagiles! . . . Tintagiles! . . . What have you done? . . . Give him back, give him back! . . . for the love of God, give him back to me! . . . I can hear nothing. . . . What are you doing with him? . . . You will not hurt him? . . . He is only a little child. . . He cannot resist. . . Look, look! . . . I mean no harm . . . I am on my knees. . . Give him back to us, I beg of you. . . . Not for my sake only, you know it well. . . I will do anything. . . I bear no ill-will, you see. . . I implore you with clasped hands. . . I was wrong. . . I am quite resigned, you see. . . I have lost all I had . . You should punish me some other way. . . There are so many things which would hurt me more . . . if you want to hurt me. . . You shall see. . . But this poor child has done no harm. . . What I said was not true . . . but I did not know. . . I know that you are very good. . . Surely the time for forgiveness has come! . . . He is so young and beautiful, and he is so small! . . . You must see that it cannot be! . . . He puts his little arms around your neck: his little mouth on your mouth; and God Himself could not say him nay . . . You will open the door, will you not? . . . I am asking so little . . . I want him for an instant, just for an instant. . . I

125

DEATH OF TINTAGILES ACT V.

cannot remember. . . You will understand. . . I did not have time. . . He can get through the tiniest opening . . . It is not difficult. . . . (*A long inexorable silence.*) . . . Monster! . . . Monster! . . . Curse you! Curse you! . . . I spit on you!

[*She sinks down and continues to sob softly, her arms outspread against the gate, in the gloom.*

MODERN PLAYS

EDITED BY

R. BRIMLEY JOHNSON AND N. ERICHSEN

MESSRS DUCKWORTH & CO. have pleasure in announcing that they have arranged to issue a series of MODERN PLAYS.

It is the aim of this series to represent, as widely as possible, the activity of the modern drama—not confined to stage performance—in England and throughout the continent of Europe. It so happens that, though translations seem to be more in demand every day, the greater number of the Continental dramatists are at present little known in this country. Among them will be found predecessors and followers of Ibsen or Maeterlinck; as well as others who reflect more independently the genius of their own country

Love's Comedy, which marks a transition from the early romantic to the later social plays, is the only important work of Ibsen's not yet translated into English. The name of Strindberg, whose position in Sweden may be compared to that of Ibsen in Norway, will be almost new to the English public. Villiers' *La Révolte* is a striking forecast of *The Doll's House*. Verhaeren is already known here as one of the foremost of Belgian writers, who, like Maeterlinck, uses the French tongue; and Brieux is among the most attractive of the younger native French dramatists. Ostrovsky's *The Storm*, painting "The Dark World," is generally recognised as *the* characteristic Russian drama. *The Convert*, by Stepniak, will be specially interesting as its author's only dramatic attempt.

The work of translation has been entrusted to English writers specially conversant with the literature represented, who, in many cases, are already associated in the public mind with the authors they are here interpreting. Every play will be translated *in extenso*, and, if in verse, as nearly as possible in the original metres. The volumes will contain brief introductions, bibliographical and explanatory rather than critical, and such annotations as may be necessary.

The volumes will be printed in small quarto, and they will cost, as a rule, 2s. 6d. net or 3s. 6d. net each.

3 HENRIETTA ST., COVENT GARDEN, W.C.   1899

EARLY VOLUMES

EMILE VERHAEREN
"Les Aubes" ("The Dawn").—Arthur Symons
3s. 6d. net.

OSTROVSKY
"The Storm."—Constance Garnett
3s. 6d. net.

MAURICE MAETERLINCK
"Intérieur."—William Archer
"La Mort de Tintagiles."
"Alladine et Palomides." }—Alfred Sutro
3s. 6d. net.

HENRIK IBSEN
"Love's Comedy" (*Kjærlighedens Komedie*).
—Prof. C. H. Herford

VILLIERS DE L'ISLE ADAM
"La Révolte."
"L'Evasion." }—Theresa Barclay

SERGIUS STEPNIAK
"The Convert."—Constance Garnett

AUGUST STRINDBERG
"The Father" (*Fadren*).—N. Erichsen

BRIEUX
"Les Bienfaiteurs."—Lucas Malet

HENRYK SIENKIEWICZ
"On a Single Card."—E. L. Voynich

Arrangements are also in progress with representative dramatists of Germany, Spain, Italy, and other countries. Further translations have been promised by Dr Garnett, Messrs Walter Leaf, Justin Huntly MacCarthy, G. A. Greene, etc.

Lightning Source UK Ltd.
Milton Keynes UK
UKHW03n1307060918
328375UK00004B/337/P